The Greenback-Labor Movement in Pennsylvania

by

RALPH R. RICKER

Published by
PENNSYLVANIA HERITAGE, INC.
BELLEFONTE, PA.

Published with the assistance of a grant-in-aid
from the Pennsylvania Historical and Museum Commission

TABLE OF CONTENTS

FOREWORD

This study by Dr. Ralph R. Ricker was a doctoral dissertation at The Pennsylvania State University, submitted in June, 1955. I had a somewhat personal interest in the study, because I suggested it as a product of some work I did myself at an earlier date on the 1896 election in Pennsylvania. At that time I was impressed by the extent and vigor of Populism in Pennsylvania and became acquainted with some of its backgrounds in what was generally looked upon as an industrial state with no agrarian movement or concern. As I learned more also of the labor movement in Pennsylvania in the era following the Civil War, it seemed to me that too little attention was paid to third party and progressive movements in the commonwealth. The major emphasis in Pennsylvania political history was entirely centered on Republicans and Democrats and the political boss and machine so strongly evident in the Republican Party.

For that reason, I urged Dr. Ricker to publish his study and make it more widely available. It is a significant contribution, in my opinion, not only to Pennsylvania history, but to the total knowledge of national political forces and movements in this very important era when the first strivings of modern progressivism resulted from the clash of interests and forces generated in the changing America of the seventies, eighties, and nineties.

While such studies are available from university libraries on microfilm, it has never been my experience that they receive very wide attention and use in this form. A published book is much more available and more apt to receive the extended attention and use which such important state and/or regional studies deserve. It has been said that history repeats itself and historians repeat each other. There is necessarily much truth in this allegation, because it is only from usable studies of special phases of history as research projects that the general historian can accumulate the material needed to make new viewpoints and information available in texts or in general histories of the country. It is my belief, as I have said, that Dr. Ricker's work is a genuine contribution.

S. K. STEVENS
Executive Director
Pennsylvania Historical and
Museum Commission

PREFACE

The purpose of this study is to trace the history and to show the significance of the Greenback-Labor Party in Pennsylvania. The Greenback-Labor political movement is frequently regarded as a phenomenon restricted, or peculiar to, the West. This, the writer believes, is an inaccurate appraisal. Evidence will be presented to demonstrate that the movement also had great importance in the East and that in Pennsylvania, especially, the Greenback-Labor Party reached a far greater stature than is usually recognized.

The first three chapters of this study are devoted to a historical review of currency in the United States, to a survey of economic conditons among laborers and farmers in Pennsylvania and in the nation, and to a brief study of the forces which prompted the rise of the Greenback-Labor Party. Subsequent chapters trace the Greenback and Greenback-Labor movement in Pennsylvania from its inception in 1876 to its incorporation with the Union-Labor movement in 1887. Local, state, and national political events related to the Greenback-Labor movement are discussed, with special emphasis being placed upon conditions, men, and sections of Pennsylvania that gave impetus to the Greenback movement. Extensive and detailed treatment is given to conventions, campaigns, and elections which had special significance. A concluding chapter attempts a re-appraisal of the Greenback-Labor movement in the light of evidence presented in this paper.

Biographical information concerning the more important leaders in the movement is supplied in the text; pertinent facts concerning lesser figures will be found in the footnotes. An attempt has been made to keep lists of party committees, candidates, election results, and related information to a minimum; only such data as provide a definite basis for inference have been included.

This study of economic distress and the resultant rallying of farmers and laborers to the support of a third political party attempts to shed some light on a political movement and a period in Pennsylvania history which, to date, has been somewhat neglected. The writer hopes he has supplied a more accurate statement showing the significance and the distribution of Greenback-Labor Party strength than has heretofore been achieved, and has presented a more clearly defined picture of the Greenback-Labor movement in Pennsylvania than has been drawn in the past.

vii

CHAPTER I

A SURVEY OF
CURRENCY PROBLEMS IN THE UNITED STATES

The problem of determining the nature and amount of circulating currency needed for efficient operation of the economy has presented itself repeatedly to Americans almost from the inception of the colonies. The demands of trade, the exigencies of war, the stresses upon the national economy—crises real and imagined, local and national—have produced situations which seemed to call for modifications and changes in the currency supply. The result has been a series of episodes of experimentation, manipulation, and improvisation that have made the history of currency in the United States a stormy one. Although this history is too lengthy and complex to be covered in detail, some knowledge of earlier currency problems and of resultant courses of action is necessary to an understanding of the political manifestations of the Greenback movement.

The colonists who came to North America were accustomed to doing business in English coins of gold and silver; however, trading activities soon introduced Spanish, Dutch and French coins. This circulation of foreign money side by side with English pieces gave rise to complex problems of price determination and cross currency valuation. Each colony acted independently in evaluating foreign money and some colonies over-evaluated foreign coins to attract them, so that currencies varied from colony to colony. The specie shortages and the need for more money for trade expansion soon gave rise to paper currency issues. Massachusetts was first with its bills of credit, issued in 1690. These were to circulate as a medium of exchange whose "value is equal to money" and would be accepted by the colony's Treasurer for all public payments.[1]

In the eighteenth century all colonies issued paper currency; either the colonial government issued bills of credit or government

---

[1] William J. Shultz and M. R. Caine, *Financial Development of the United States*, 13.

"banks" issued currency bills to citizens upon real or personal security. Pennsylvania's public loan bank furnishes an interesting example of the issue of a paper currency authorized by a colonial government. Pennsylvania's legislature in 1723, after a severe depression attributed to a lack of a circulating medium, established a loan office governed by four commissioners who were empowered to issue and loan bills of small denomination, the largest not to exceed twenty shillings. The security had to be land of double the value loaned, together with a bond and judgment on the borrower's whole establishment, with the condition that one-twelfth of the sum should be annually paid back at five per cent interest. Not less than twenty pounds and not more than 200 pounds could be loaned to any person. Pennsylvania's plan was so successfully managed that another fund was established in 1739 to run for sixteen years.[2]

The British government did not look with favor upon colonial currency experiments, but neither was it totally blind to the colonies' need for circulating media. Since specie currency in sufficient quantities to keep the channels of commerce moving was lacking, the British government permitted the colonies to print paper money. This was a more expedient, and a cheaper solution than furnishing them with a metallic currency. In the first half of the eighteenth century Britain contented itself with trying to regulate rather than to prohibit paper currency, but finally, in 1751, the New England colonies were forbidden to issue any further legal tender bills of credit or "bank notes" except to cover current expenses and war costs. This exception was used by Connecticut to issue 346,500 pounds worth of new bills of credit between 1755 and 1763. The Parliamentary Act of 1751 may have stifled economic expansion of the New England colonies, but it had a stabilizing effect on their currencies. Such non-legal-tender bills of credit as were issued thereafter were honored when due, and they circulated without depreciation.

Prior to 1751, New York, New Jersey, and Pennsylvania had exercised moderation in their currency policy and, after 1751, became even more conservative. This was not true in the southern colonies. Bills of credit based on warehouse receipts were freely issued, particularly in Virginia where over 400,000 pounds worth

[2] Davis R. Dewey, *Financial History of the United States*, 27.

of bills of credit were issued between 1755 and 1760. Many of these freely emitted bills fell to ten percent of their value within a year. These excessive issues in the South goaded Parliament in 1764 to extend the Act of 1751 to all colonies and removed the war finance exception,[3] a policy which did not promote happiness among the commercially-minded colonists.

At the outbreak of the Revolution the nation was faced with a difficult financial problem; only $4,000,000 in specie was in circulation, a little less than $1.50 per person. With foreign loans unavailable at this time, and state paper currency depreciated, Congress was forced to try to finance the War with a paper currency of its own. The first financial act of the Second Continental Congress was to issue $6,000,000 in bills of credit, commonly called continental currency. Congress had no means of redeeming the bills, but placed them into circulation and provided, without any authority, that the continental issues would be redeemed by the States in proportion to their population after four years. In order to keep the continental notes from depreciating too rapidly, Congress several times urged the States to redeem their quotas of the currency outstanding but the States failed to act. By 1779, $241,552,780 of continental currency had been issued and the value of the dollar had fallen to three cents. The money had lost its purchasing power and Congress was ridiculed for issuing it. The leaders of Congress, realizing that further issues would be suicidal, resolved in 1779 to print no more.[4]

After several attempts at stabilizing this paper currency had failed, the Confederation government established the Bank of North America as a means of steadying the financial picture. The Bank opened on January 7, 1782, and functioned successfully by making short-term loans to merchants, by discounting foreign bills of exchange for the government, and by making short-term loans to it. Its bank notes were readily accepted in transactions because they were redeemable upon presentation. The success of the Bank of North America led to the establishment in 1784 of the Bank of Massachusetts and the Bank of New York. All three banks were combinations of commercial banks and governmental institutions. Each bank was to be the sole banking

---

[3] Shultz and Caine, *Financial Development*, 33-36.
[4] Dewey, *Financial History*, 37.

institution for the State. It was to receive funds on deposit and transfer them by check or draft. It was to make loans on promissory notes, with or without security backing, and might pay out the loaned funds in its own bank notes. The bank notes of these three banks were another variety of paper currency in circulation before 1789. The success of these banks led to the establishment of private commercial banks. By 1800 twenty-nine banking corporations had been formed—twelve in New England, nine in the Middle States, and five in the Southern States.[5]

During the 1780's continental paper currency and State bills of credit continued in slight circulation but their depreciation was so great that they served as a medium of speculation rather than as a medium of exchange. During the specie shortage of 1785-1786, seven States issued additional paper currency. North Carolina issued bills of credit. New York, South Carolina, New Jersey, Rhode Island, Pennsylvania and Georgia made government bank issues—paper money issued not for governmental expenses, but for loans to citizens upon their lands or other securities. Since this currency was not made legal tender, no great harm was done to creditors.

After the success of the Bank of North America, the Confederation government in 1785 attempted to further stabilize currency by establishing a new dollar of 375 64/100 grains of silver and making the ratio of gold and silver 15 to 1. The old coinage divisions of 90ths were dropped and a decimal system was established in its place, with a copper one-half cent, silver dime, a silver half dollar, a silver dollar, a gold eagle (ten dollars) and a gold double eagle (twenty dollars). None of these were minted during the Confederation period, and not until 1794 was a United States mint established using this system of coinage. By 1800 it had produced only $700,000 in gold pieces, $1,200,000 in silver and $50,000 in copper. Because of the scarcity of American coins, the legal tender status of foreign coins was not suspended until 1802.[6]

With the establishment of the new government in 1789, the financial problem was one of the first attacked. The Office of Secretary of the Treasury was established and a refunding plan for

[5] Margaret C. Myers, *The New York Money Market*, 17.
[6] Shultz and Caine, *Financial Development*, 87.

the $79,000,000 debt was adopted. The first United States Bank, created by the Act of February 14, 1791, was chartered for twenty years. The bank's charter contained definite limitation on its lending activities. Loans could be effected by creating deposits or issuing bank notes; these notes were not legal tender but were receivable for dues at the Federal Treasury.[7]

Between 1800-1815, two hundred eight state banks were chartered, whose total paper bank note issues were $45,500,000. With the demise of the first United States Bank in 1811 and with the advent of the War in 1812, the United States was without a stable currency. Specie became scarce during the conflict and state banks, to fill the void, issued $17,500,000 of new paper currency. The faults and limitations of State bank notes were accentuated by the War. In many States there were few or no restrictions on their issue. In many cases, State bank issues circulated at par in restricted localities where some possibility of redemption existed. Loans were often made in State bank notes with the stipulation that the loan could not be repaid in the bank's own notes. Over one hundred banks had to suspend specie payments by 1814. The Government, trying to finance a war with State bank notes, was forced to issue Treasury notes; Congress voted $30,500,000 in Treasury note issues bearing five and two-fifths percent interest. These notes circulated in denominations of twenty dollars, fifty dollars, and one hundred dollars and were retired by 1818 when interest on the notes ceased.[8]

Immediately after the War ended, agitation for a new United States Bank increased, but one was not chartered until April, 1816, because of opposition of western and southern Republicans. The Bank was chartered for twenty years, with a capitalization of $35,000,000, and was designed to serve as a depository for Federal funds, to make loans, and to issue notes in denominations of five dollars or higher to a total of $35,000,000. The progress of the Bank was rapid in the decade of the 1820's, and by 1828 it had $51,000,000 on loan; a $9,900,000 note circulation; $6,200,000 in specie; $6,000,000 on deposit; and paid a seven percent dividend. By 1830, $61,000,000 in State bank notes circulated; business ex-

[7] Dewey, *Financial History*, 98-101.
[8] Shultz and Caine, *Financial Development*, 145, 157-161.

pansion increased them in 1837 to $149,000,000, with only $45,-000,000 in specie in the banks to support the notes.[9]

The operation of the Second United States Bank aroused resentment among both liberals and conservatives. The liberals—who wanted a greater currency inflation—were farmers, eastern and western operators of State banks, speculators, and business leaders in the West and South.[10] They protested against the control of the State-chartered banks exerted by the United States Bank when it would set high discount rates on the notes of a State bank which it believed had issued more currency than its reserves justified. This and other policies of the Bank had the effect of keeping the State banks in line and prevented them from issuing the inflated dollars wanted by speculators.

The financial conservatives were found largely among the eastern workingmen with some support from small southern farmers.[11] They opposed the Bank because they believed their problem of high prices and low wages was caused by an inflated currency manipulated by the Bank for the benefit of the upper classes. Their solution was to abolish paper currency, except in large denominations needed for business, and to return to a gold and silver basis for payment of debts and wages. This was impossible as long as the Bank of the United States ruled the finances of the country. Jackson believed the greatest evil of the Bank was not the curbing of state bank issues but the over-issue of its own bank notes, which made it all-powerful.[12]

After Jackson's re-election in 1832, he took steps to curb the Bank by withdrawing Federal funds on deposit there and by placing the funds in State banks, using in all eighty-nine. Many of these banks used these Federal funds as security for land loans. This action led to financial catastrophe for these banks after the Federal Government issued the Specie Circular and passed the Surplus Act of 1836. The first required specie payment for government land, and the second distributed the federal surplus to the States. This surplus on deposit in State banks had to be returned. Since many banks had no other means of recovering their surplus except to recall loans, disaster resulted for the banks and

[9] *Ibid.*, 202.
[10] Arthur M. Schlesinger, Jr., *The Age of Jackson*, 78.
[11] *Ibid.*, 79.
[12] Ray A. Billington, *Westward Expansion*, 360, 361.

borrowers. By mid-1837 only a few of over seven hundred State banks were able to make specie payments. A major depression followed from which the nation did not fully recover until 1843.

The income of the Federal Government decreased during the depression, and for the second time since 1789 it was necessary to issue Treasury notes to keep Government finances operating. By 1843 a total of $43,000,000 of Treasury notes had been voted but rarely did more than $10,000,000 circulate in any year, as they were issued for only one year at six percent interest.[13] The Government, in 1846, after the recent experience with State banking, decided to reestablish an Independent Treasury[14] through which the Government "became its own banker."[15]

State regulations on issuance of bank paper currency increased in the 1840's with the adoption by many states of the New York Free Banking Law of 1838. This law ended the creation of banks by charter. Anyone willing to comply with the bank laws was free to open a bank. "Free" bank notes were printed, not by the banks, but by the state comptroller. To obtain notes, the banks deposited with the comptroller federal bonds, state bonds, or mortgages on improved real estate.

In the 1850's the discovery of gold in California increased specie circulation by $88,000,000. This increased specie circulation was not enough to meet increased business demands, and the increased use of the bank check as a complement to the bank note resulted, with the attendant growth of clearing houses where banks cancelled their mutual obligations. By 1857, fifteen hundred State banks had issued $214,778,822 in State bank notes.

The opening of the Civil War found the Union Treasury $100,000,000 in debt. Not for fifty years had the Treasury been so poorly prepared to take on the financial burdens of a war. Secretary of the Treasury Salmon P. Chase attempted to follow the precepts which Albert Gallatin had laid down in 1812 and which the government resumed in 1846, "Finance your war costs on borrowed funds, and increase your taxes only for the purpose of covering service on the newly-incurred debt." Congress did

[13] Shultz and Caine, *Financal Development*, 233.
[14] The first independent treasury, advocated by President Van Buren, was established in 1840 but it existed less than a year before Congress abolished it. *Ibid.*, 263.
[15] Esther R. Taus, *Central Banking Functions of the United States Treasury, 1789-1941*, 50.

not pass a tax measure to help finance the War until July 1, 1862, but attempted in July, 1861, to raise $150,000,000 for war finance by issuing the "7.30" three-year bonds. Popular sale of the "7.30" bonds was not a success; only 45 million dollars' worth were sold to the public. The remainder were taken over by the Eastern banks with the hope of selling them to their clients. The Treasury insisted on being paid in specie and the banks insisted this policy would strip them of gold. The banks proved to be good prophets. The New York banks suspended specie payment on December 30, 1861, and the Government was forced off a specie basis.

The Treasury was in a dilemma. With specie hoarded, State banks unwilling or unable to cooperate with the Treasury, and Congress not yet ready to pass a National Banking Act some other means had to be devised quickly to meet the mounting expenses. Treasury notes to circulate as a national medium of exchange seemed to be the solution. Treasury notes had been issued on four previous occasions: in 1812, 1837, 1846, and by Congress under the loan acts of June, 1860, and February, 1861. These previous Treasury note issues were given short terms and bore interest. They were used by the government to make payments and could be converted into bonds, and their use as a currency was discouraged. The issue of Treasury notes—the famous Greenbacks—voted in February, 1862, did not carry interest and was made full legal tender except for payment of custom dues and debt interest. Three issues of these notes, totalling $450,000,000, were authorized and circulated during the War. Their value fluctuated with the fortunes of war and with the speculative price of gold on the exchanges. On July 1, 1864, when an act to close the gold exchanges raised distrust of the Government's policies, Greenbacks were worth thirty-five cents on the dollar. By the spring of 1865 Greenback value was back to seventy-five cents. Subsidiary silver coinage also disappeared during the War, and the Treasury, to check the use of postage stamps for money, issued on March 3, 1863, fractional paper notes of five, ten, twenty-five, and fifty cents to a total of $30,000,000.

At the urging of Secretary Chase the idea of a Federal-chartered banking system gained favor as the War progressed, culminating in the National Bank Acts of 1863 and 1864. These acts provided that commercial banking institutions could be incorporated under

Federal charter and be subject exclusively to Federal control. Every National Bank had to deposit Federal bonds with the comptroller of the currency; such deposit had to equal one-third of the bank's capital, and not less than $30,000. In return the bank received notes printed by the Federal Government to the extent of ninety percent of the market value, not exceeding par, of the bonds. If a bank defaulted, the comptroller could sell the bonds and reimburse the note holders. The banks provided the United States with a uniform currency, and the bond collateral assured the Government of a new market for bonds. In 1865, the ten percent tax on State bank notes drove them out of existence and caused over seven hundred State banks to take out National Bank charters. By January 1, 1866, sixteen hundred National Banks had been organized, with $150,000,000 in National Bank notes circulating largely as a replacement for the withdrawn State bank notes.[16] Thus the United States emerged from the Civil War with a paper currency made up of National Bank notes, Greenbacks, and fractional money.

It was this paper currency that became the central issue of the great struggle over the National monetary policy in the fifteen years after the war.

[16] Shultz and Caine, *Financial Development*, 318-324.

CHAPTER II

THE STATE OF
POLITICS, LABOR, AND AGRICULTURE AFTER 1865

Politically the period after 1865 has been characterized as one in which political morality was practically nonexistent—a time when the political spoilsmen were in control:

> In business and politics the captains of industry did their work boldly, blandly, and cynically. Exploiting workers and milking farmers, bribing congressmen, buying legislatures, spying upon competitors, hiring armed guards, dynamiting property, using threats and intrigue and force, they made a mockery of the ideals of the simple gentry who imagined that the nation's development could take place with dignity and restraint under the regime of laissez-faire.[1]

The political parties in the post-Civil War period were interested in power and spoils, not principles and issues. To finance its continuance in power, the Republican Party levied assessments on Federal officeholders, plundered custom house receipts, made fraudulent extortions from importers, and expected large contributions from the recipients of government favors. The opening of three billion acres of land in the West presented a whole new area for special favors and brought a besieging crowd of lobbyists to Washington seeking land grants, subsidies, and freedom from regulatory legislation. For these favors capitalists or their agents supplied campaign funds and furnished the politicians with investment opportunities.[2] Large sums were spent on bribes: the Central Pacific Railroad, between 1875 and 1885, spent as much as $500,000 annually to buy favors.[3]

After the inauguration of Congressional Reconstruction and the Presidential Impeachment episode, this "saturnalia of plunder"[4]

[1] Richard Hofstadter, *The American Political Tradition and the Men Who Made It,* 162.
[2] Matthew Josephson, *The Politicos, 1865-1896,* 102-107.
[3] *Ibid.,* 168.
[4] *Ibid.,* 101.

went into high gear in the Grant administration and lasted until 1881. President Grant possessed neither the experience nor the will to stem the materialistic trend in politics. A new generation of political leaders took over Congress: Roscoe Conkling of New York, James G. Blaine of Maine, General Benjamin F. Butler of Massachusetts, William D. Kelley and Samuel J. Randall of Pennsylvania, James Garfield of Ohio—all aided and abetted by certain older political leaders like Simon Cameron of Pennsylvania, Zachariah Chandler of Michigan, and Oliver P. Morton of Indiana.[5] Together they hastened the exploitation of the nation's resources through grants and subsidies.

Grant's administration was noted for the poor calibre of men chosen to fill Federal posts, and this fact, coupled with the action of certain leaders, soon cast a blemish on his administration. In 1873 investigation by a committee of the House and Senate revealed that a number of congressmen had been given free shares of stock in the Credit Mobilier, the construction company for the Union Pacific Railroad, a company that had received over ten million acres of land and a heavy cash subsidy. The House of Representatives accepted the view of the committee that most of the congressmen implicated had acted without corrupt motive or purpose.[6] A long series of scandal followed. Secretary of Treasury William A. Richardson resigned in 1873 over diversion of Treasury Department funds, particularly over Custom House collections in Boston.[7] In 1875 the exposure of the Whisky Ring brought to light another fraud. The Post Office Department had its Star Route Frauds, and in the War Department it was shown that Secretary William Belknap had lived for years upon the proceeds of the sale of army trading posts. When prominent citizens made a complaint to Senator Conklin or Senator Cameron, they would "encounter only a shrug of the shoulders, a laugh."[8]

A minority in Congress led by Carl Schurz, Charles Sumner, and Lyman Trumbull protested against the character of political affairs. They advocated tariff and civil service reform and attacked the administration's morals. A Liberal Republican movement to block the re-election of Grant started in 1872, with many prominent

[5] *Ibid.*, 164.
[6] Allan Nevins, *The Emergence of Modern America, 1865-1878*, 188-190.
[7] Robert S. Holzman, *Stormy Ben Butler*, 208.
[8] Josephson, *Politicos*, 177.

non-political leaders enrolled in the organization—men of the calibre of Henry Adams, Charles Francis Adams, William Cullen Bryant, Charles W. Eliot, and Horace White. This liberal group haggled over principles and a candidate and finally nominated Horace Greely, a Republican high tariff protectionist, who was later endorsed by the Democrats. Greeley's nomination caused many liberals and Democrats to stay away from the polls and Grant was easily re-elected. Political reform had failed and the "Stalwart" Republican spoilsmen were able to continue to control the government until 1884, when dissident Republicans supported the Democratic reform candidate, Grover Cleveland, and in certain key areas such as New York were credited with being determining factors in his election.[9]

During the exposure of maladministration and graft in the Grant era, the Republican leaders did not seem overly fearful of the "honest masses" of the party. What concerned them was the serious objections raised by the respectable and affluent elements who had always supported the party.[10] This lack of consideration influenced many voters among the farmers and workingmen to cast their votes for the Greenback-Labor Party's candidates after 1876.

Rutherford B. Hayes succeeded to the Presidency in 1877 after the well-known Eight to Seven Electorial Commission vote. His administration was marked by four years of brawling with "stalwart" Republican leaders over political reform which soon led to the administration of a President-without-a-party.[11] Hayes served during the height of violent conflicts between captains of industry and railroad barons as they struggled for the continental market for steel, oil, and transportation. Unstable economic conditions heightened by labor violence which necessitated the use of Federal troops to put down the violence and the rise of the National Greenback-Labor Party as a protest against the conservative financial policies of the Republicans are all part of the picture of the Hays administration.[12] The picture changed little in the Garfield-Arthur administration except for improved eco-

---

[9] Hofstadter, *American Political Traditions,* 176.
[10] Josephson, *Politicos,* 205.
[11] H. J. Eckenrode, *Rutherford B. Hayes,* 284-303.
[12] Josephson, *Politicos,* 240-267.

nomic conditions and the passage of the Pendleton Civil Service Act.

Realization of the enormity of the political malefaction during this period becomes all the more acute when one considers the difficulties of two large segments of the electorate—the laborers and the farmers. Despite a general industrial growth, agricultural expansion, and numerous increases in national wealth in the post-Civil War period, the lot of the individual laborer and farmer, except for isolated instances of a temporary nature, was not a happy one.

During the Civil War rising prices and lagging wages were the workingmen's first concern. The chart below reveals the situation in stark figures:[13]

Year	Prices in Currency	Prices in Gold	Money Wages in Currency	Money Wages in Gold
1860	100.0	100.0	100.0	100.0
1861	100.6	100.6	100.8	100.8
1862	117.8	114.9	102.9	100.4
1863	148.6	102.4	110.5	76.2
1864	190.5	122.5	125.6	80.8
1865	216.8	100.3	143.1	66.2

To help their cause laboring men had organized into unions and had struck for wages comparable to living costs. In 1863 the conductors and horsecar drivers in New York, the union printers of St. Louis, and carpenters, painters, and plumbers in almost every city went on strike for higher wages. The iron moulders sought a fifteen percent increase. Shipwrights, longshoremen, and. locomotive engineers called out their members in various areas. Workingmen received their first substantial increases, but the rapidly rising prices afforded them small relief and the movement was renewed the next year. As a result of the struggle labor's strength increased; between 1863 and 1864 the number of trade unions rose from 79 to 270, with a membership of over 200,000. Of these unions, 32 organized on a nationwide basis.[14] The most prominent national unions were the reorganized Iron Moulders' International, the Machinists, the Blacksmiths, the Locomotive

[13] Harold U. Faulkner, *American Economic History*, 345.
[14] Foster R. Dulles, *Labor in America*, 93.

Engineers, the American Miners, and the Sons of Vulcan (iron puddlers). Labor publications such as Fincher's *Trades' Review* revived and increased in number.

The War made it clear that labor, to meet the challenge presented by growing national industries, would have to organize on a nationwide basis so that it could better present and protect its interests against the growing power of management. After the War, the number and strength of craft unions increased and two national unions were formed: the National Labor Union, founded in 1866, made up of national, state, and local organizations; and the Knights of Labor, formed in 1869, on the principle of one union for all producers.[15] Labor organizations after the War espoused various causes which they thought would help them to improve their economic status; they formed eight-hour leagues, studied and experimented with consumer cooperatives for the workingmen, advocated currency reform, protested against the growth of monopolies and factory working conditions. These goals they hoped to attain by legislation.

This post-war effort seemed to bring some gains, but the depression of 1873 repeated the old story of falling prices, business stagnation, curtailed production, wage cuts, and unemployment. As factories and mines closed or curtailed production, some three million men were thrown out of work. Hard times not only brought to an end attempted national labor unity but also almost completely shattered the existing national craft unions. By 1877, only nine of thirty national unions were in existence, and union membership had fallen from 300,000 to 50,000.[16]

During the depression workingmen were unorganized, often unemployed, and frequently in extreme want. The fight to better their economic lot seemed hopeless. Frustration and misery made many desperate and bitter, feelings that culminated in the violent railroad strikes of 1877. Violence subsided with the intervention of Federal troops, but these events left the laboring man with a new and clearer realization of the need for reorganization and a new approach to his problem. The National Labor Union in 1872 had failed in its attempt to organize an independent political party. Again after 1875 many labor leaders decided that they could not

---

[15] Joseph Dorfman, *The Economic Mind in American Civilization, 1865-1918*, III, 125.
[16] Dulles, *Labor in America*, 112.

depend upon the older parties for a sympathetic solution to their grievances; this realization led many of them to the conclusion that labor, to gain its goals, would have to organize another independent political movement.

These generally poor conditions in the labor world were compounded in Pennsylvania, where manufacturing had replaced agriculture as the dominant industry. During the depression, lay-offs and wage cuts among the coal miners, the iron and steel workers, and the railroad employees steadily increased. The decline in wages among these groups after 1875 can be seen in the following table:

AVERAGE DAILY WAGE IN PENNSYLVANIA[17]

	1875	1877	1878	1880
Anthracite miners (contract)	$3.00	$1.91	$1.97	$2.71
Anthracite laborers (inside)	2.00	1.69	1.38	1.62
Anthracite laborers (outside)	1.65	1.47	1.21	1.30
Anthracite drivers	1.64	1.62	1.30	1.26
Bituminous miners	2.47	1.65	1.88	2.25
Bituminous laborers (inside)	1.90	1.64	1.47	1.69
Bituminous laborers (outside)	1.76	1.34	1.47	1.46
Bituminous drivers	1.81	1.57	1.46	1.63
Iron moulders	2.33	2.12	1.83	1.84
Boiler-makers	2.66	2.00	1.87	2.14
Pattern-makers	2.45	2.27	1.62	1.99
Foundry laborers	1.60	1.25	1.06	1.16

It should be noted that the low point of wages in Pennsylvania was reached in 1877 and 1878. Even though labor protested violently its 1877 wage cuts by striking, the strikes were unsuccessful in raising wages. Wages were lower in 1878 than in 1877 and did not increase appreciably until 1880 when economic conditions had improved.

Pennsylvania workmen had many grievances in addition to scarcity of employment and low wages. Chief among them was the practice of paying wages in kind. The so-called "truck," or company store system was in vogue particularly among the mine operators and some iron and steel companies. Under this system, the employees received their pay at irregular intervals in store orders. The pay practices of management and the lack of respect for its agreements with workingmen on this subject are obvious

[17] "Industrial Statistics," *Annual Report of the Secretary of Internal Affairs of the Commonwealth of Pennsylvania*, III (1880-81), Leg. Doc. No. 8, 160, 163, 165.

in the account of the strike of 1,000 employees of the Erie Railroad at the Susquehanna Depot, Susquehanna County, on March 2, 1874:

> The railroad company failed to make regular pay days for several months, keeping the men from a month to six weeks without their earnings. For the month of October 1873, they were paid December 2, and on January 15, 1874, they received their November earnings, and their December earnings were paid on February 7. The men demanded a regular pay day. After being out six hours their request was granted, and the company, through their general supervisor of motive power, signed an agreement to the effect that they would pay the hands on or before the 15th of each month for all labor performed in the month preceding.

On the next day, March 3, the paymaster arrived and paid all employees for January. On March 15 the employees were notified they would have to wait for their pay until the roadmen received their January pay before they would receive pay for February. On March 25, the men all stopped work. They stopped the freight trains by removing parts of the engines, disabling forty-five locomotives. On March 27, passenger trains were not allowed to run. "They [the railroad workers] claimed if the company had a right to keep their money one month they had an equal right to stop the company's trains until they were paid." The strike was settled by the company's paying the February and March wages, with the added condition that the company would rehire only "such men as they think are for their interest." About eight hundred men were re-employed by April 2, but the settlement illustrated that it did not pay to be on a labor grievance committee, because it was reported that "the committee without exception were refused employment."[18]

Increasing production demands at the same pay rates, use of strikebreakers, and the substitution of labor-saving devices were other problems faced by Pennsylvania labor. An example of the latter occurred in June, 1877, when the lamp chimney blowers struck in three Pittsburgh factories over the introduction of the patent "crimper," a machine operated by steam power for crimping the top of lamp chimneys. The machine increased the output,

[18] "Labor Troubles in Pennsylvania," *Annual Report of the Secretary of Internal Affairs*, III (1881), 309.

but the company wished to pay the same wages as before. The blowers objected and refused to work, "alleging that the increased production was injurious to their trade."[19] The strike was not settled until June, 1879.

Agriculture, like industry, received a tremendous stimulus as a result of the Civil War. Production of all farm products increased, particularly corn, wheat, hogs, and sheep. Prices increased on farm products, but they did not keep pace with the increase in price of commodities purchased, as shown by the report that wholesale farm prices rose 75 points during the War while wholesale commodity prices rose 100 points.[20]

After the War ended, the farmers, particularly those in the South and West, were harassed by several major problems: overproduction and falling prices, a deflated currency, a lack of credit, debts and high interest rates, high railroad rates, and monopoly prices on many of the products that they had to buy. The income actually received by farmers in the West and in the cotton belt was foremost in the list of causes of distress and unrest. The farmers complained that they received only a small portion of the wholesale price. With corn selling for $1.00 a bushel in New York, it was hard for them to understand why they received but ten cents a bushel in Kansas. In their desire to find a scapegoat they blamed their financial difficulties on the railroads. The farmers of Kansas, Nebraska, and Iowa plaintively maintained that it cost a bushel of corn to send another bushel to market. The Minnesota wheat farmers said the same of wheat.

Another complaint was that the farmers had little part in fixing the price of the products they sold and no part in fixing the price of the goods they bought. They inveighed against monopolies and trusts. Westerners complained specifically against the prices paid by the beef trust and against the prices charged by the plow trust, the barbed wire trust, and the farm machinery trust, while the southern farmer complained of the fertilizer trust, the jute-bagging trust, and a cottonseed trust.[21] Both farm elements tried to counteract the trust influence with buying cooperatives and state legislation, but met with little success.

In the northeastern part of the United States farmers enjoyed a period of relative prosperity after the war which was to last

[19] *Ibid.*, 321.
[20] Fred A. Shannon, *The Farmer's Last Frontier*, 94.
[21] John D. Hicks, *The Populist Revolt*, 60-95.

until early 1868. Many of the poor farms in this section had been abandoned, and the former farmer had moved west or had joined the labor force of expanding industry. The farmers who remained had altered the nature of their agricultural production from grain, wool, and beef to dairying, vegetable and fruit growing.[22] It was

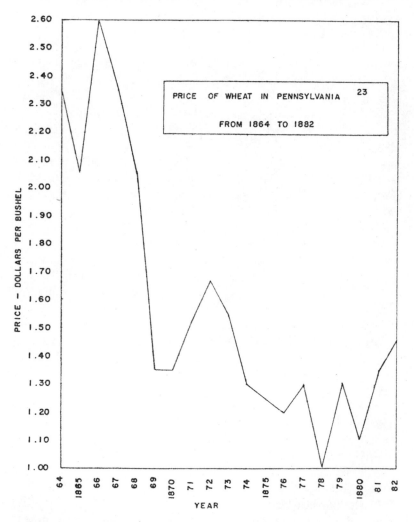

PRICE OF WHEAT IN PENNSYLVANIA [23]

FROM 1864 TO 1882

[22] Faulkner, *Economic History,* 218, 394.
[23] *Report of the State Board of Agriculture, Agriculture of Pennsylvania 1881,* 16.

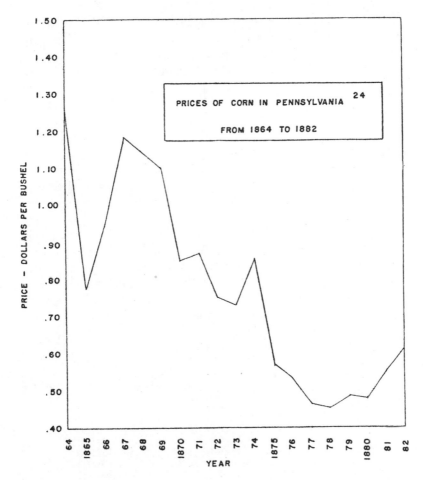

PRICES OF CORN IN PENNSYLVANIA [24]

FROM 1864 TO 1882

not until the severe drop in farm prices after 1867, followed by
the tightening of credit in the 1870's, that the eastern farmer was
severely affected, particularly in the more frontier-like areas such
as the agricultural and lumber regions in many sections of Pennsylvania's northern counties.

The severity of the price drop and the resultant distress to the
farmer can be noted in the following two charts showing the price
fluctuations of Pennsylvania's wheat and corn crops between 1864
and 1882.

[24] *Ibid.*

The causes of this decline were many. In 1881 the State Board of Agriculture blamed the situation in part upon "the close competition in the production of grain, beef, and livestock which for a number of years has existed between the eastern and western producers of these articles, and the narrow margin which is left from their production upon the high priced lands of our state."[25]

The surveys of the State Board of Agriculture revealed that from 1865 to 1880 wheat averaged only eleven to fifteen bushels per acre and corn averaged thirty to forty-two bushels per acre. The severe drop in the corn price by 1880, along with western competition, caused the Pennsylvania farmer to pay less attention to his corn crop, for in 1881 the average yield was only twenty-two bushels per acre.[26]

Although farm acreage increased in Pennsylvania by 1,220,000 acres in the decade of the 1870's, the decrease in the price of farm products was so large that the total value of farm products decreased by approximately $17,000,000. The plight of the farmers who worked hard and planted more acres and yet received less for their toil is implied in the figures cited below:

FARM PRICES AND ACREAGE 1871-1880[27]

	Annual value of Pennsylvania crops	Annual acreage under cultivation in Pennsylvania
1871	$128,495,000	5,980,000
1873	115,965,000	5,780,000
1876	104,925,000	6,700,000
1877	99,159,000	6,934,000
1878	99,654,000	7,162,000
1879	99,750,000	7,187,000
1880	111,250,000	7,200,000

The chief reason for acreage increase, cited by the State Board of Agriculture, was the "increased farming in the lumber, coal, and oil regions of the state where a partial stagnation of these interests had stimulated agriculture as a means of making a living and it was to these regions that an increase in acreage was expected in the future."[28]

[25] *Ibid.*, 30.
[26] *Ibid.* (1882), 72.
[27] *Ibid.* (1880), 23.
[28] *Ibid.*

The paradox of more land under cultivation and less income was met by many farmers by switching from cereal crops. The farmers in northern Pennsylvania switched to dairying and concentrated on butter and cheese manufacturing,[29] but the low prices prevailing everywhere resulted in low returns from their products. The fourth annual meeting of the Pennsylvania Dairymen's Association held in Meadville on January 16, 1878, reported that one-tenth of the cow population of the state was found in these northern counties, and that this section produced one-ninth of the butter and one-half of the cheese of the state. Butter prices were low at the Meadville market in 1878, varying from seven to nine cents a pound from May to August, and rising during the remainder of the year to ten and fourteen cents a pound with an occasional drop to eight cents when a large supply was presented.[30]

Pennsylvania farmers, looking for improvement economically and socially, also affiliated with the National Grange. The first active subordinate Grange was organized in 1871 at Montgomery, in Lycoming County. The State Grange was organized at Reading in 1873, with David B. Mauger as first Master. Victor E. Piollet succeeded him in 1876. At the second meeting of the State Grange, held at Williamsport on August 9, 1875, the organization included over 400 subordinate Granges and a membership of over 25,000. By 1880, Pennsylvania was one of the strongest Grange states, and in 1940 still ranked third in membership.

As in the West, the Pennsylvania Grange was not happy about the treatment the Pennsylvania farmer received from the railroads. Gerald C. Brown, State Lecturer, at the State Convention held in Harrisburg in 1886 attributed much of the decline in the value of agricultural land to their practices:

> The railroad record in Pennsylvania is monstrous. This very season the Pennsylvania Railroad has carried grain from Chicago to New York for eighty cents per ton mile

[29] The counties of Erie, Mercer, Crawford, Lawrence, and parts of Butler, Warren, and Venango are considered today the Northwestern dairy area of Pennsylvania. The counties of Potter, Tioga, Bradford, Susquehanna, and parts of Wayne, Wyoming and Lackawanna comprise the Northeastern dairy area. "Types of Farming in Pennsylvania," Extension Bulletin 479, Pennsylvania State University, 47, 48.
[30] *Report of the Pennsylvania Dairymen's Association, Agriculture of Pennsylvania, 1878,* 468.

less than it has charged from Lancaster County. It has carried grain from the Western elevators to the seaboard for two mills per ton mile while it made our farmers pay two cents per ton mile for one-tenth the distance, or 100 times as much for the same service. In ten years our Pennsylvania farms have shrunk in value $63,000,000. Farms lying along the railroad have lost most.[31]

The State Board of Agriculture estimated the 1870 to 1880 loss in market value of Pennsylvania farms at $68,000,000. The Board noted, "Berks County reports more sheriffs' sales of farm property than in any three years—no longer is it with the farmer a matter of getting rich or even making money; it has narrowed down to a struggle for a bare subsistence."[32]

With this bleak history of economic malaise—the laborer with low wages, high commodity prices, burdensome taxes and frequent periods of unemployment; the farmer with low farm produce prices, exorbitant freight rates, high interest charges on his debt —with this background, laborers and farmers were willing to subscribe to any expedient that would relieve the shortage of circulating currency. The expanded use of the Greenback appeared to offer the greatest hope. Thus, when Secretary of the Treasury Hugh McCulloch in 1865 and 1866 began retiring Greenbacks bringing the amount in circulation down to $365,000,000, the laboring men and the farmers were aroused to political action.

[31] William F. Hill, *The Grange Movement in Pennsylvania,* 7, 22, 25, 26.
[32] *Report of State Board of Agriculture, Agriculture of Pennsylvania, 1890,* 257-259.

CHAPTER III

THE BEGINNING
OF THE GREENBACK POLITICAL MOVEMENT

The first Greenback political movement began in 1866. The western farmers demanded an inflation of the currency, to be accomplished by restoring the retired Greenbacks to circulation. Various Democratic politicians in the West like Henry Clay Dean of Iowa; Allen G. Thurman, George Pendleton, and Clement L. Vallandigham of Ohio, sensing the political implications of the movement, began to demand an increased Greenback circulation with one currency for the "plough holder and the bondholder"[1] as a means of liquidating the war debt, overthrowing Republican rule, and emancipating the region from eastern economic and financial control. Currency inflation was taken up by the Cincinnati *Enquirer* as a method of wresting control of the Democratic Party from August Belmont and Tammany Hall. Spokesmen for trade unions, notable among them Congressman Samuel F. Cary, of Cincinnati, manifested interest in currency inflation as a possible solution for their problems.[2]

This original Greenback movement was put to a test in the Ohio gubernatorial election of 1867. When Rutherford B. Hayes, advocate of sound money, defeated the Democratic candidate, Allen G. Thurman—who was then elected to the United States Senate by the legislature—Ohio Democrats decided that their movement was too radical and produced a watered-down version in the form of a plan to pay the war debt with Greenbacks.[3] The Ohio Idea was so ably presented to the Democratic National Convention in 1868 that the party adopted it as its major plank. Although Republicans announced their opposition, pressure from the indebted West became so strong that Congress passed an act

[1] Reginald C. McGrane, *William Allen, A Study in Western Democracy,* 181.
[2] Chester M. Destler, *American Radicalism,* 7, 35.
[3] McGrane, *William Allen,* 179-182.

suspending the authority of the Secretary of Treasury to contract Greenbacks further.[4]

Meanwhile a second Greenback movement had developed in the
National Labor Union. The organization had been created in 1866
by trade unionists who regarded economic activity as the most
logical method of securing labor's objectives. But many of the
leaders of the National Labor Union, among them William Sylvis,
Richard F. Trevellick, and A. C. Cameron, had become interested
in Edward Kellogg's inter-convertibility scheme.[5]

Kellogg had been a successful dry goods merchant in New York
City who had been forced to suspend his business during the
panic of 1837. A few years later, after speculating successfully in
Milwaukee real estate, he retired to devote part of his time to
research on the cause of the calamity in which he and so many
others had been involved. He began his crusade for paper currency
with the publication, in 1849, of a treatise under the staggering
title, *Labor and other Capital: The Rights of Each Secured and
the Wrongs Eradicated. Or, an exposition of the cause why few
are Wealthy and many poor, and the delineation of a system,
which without infringing the rights of property, will give labor
its just reward.*[6] This work was an attempt to reconcile conflict-
ing theories and emotions regarding first, government control of
currency; second, hard money; and third, paper money or credit.

Kellogg called attention to the rapid accumulation of wealth
in the hands of a few and developed two interrelated doctrines as
a cure for the evil; the legal tender theory of money and a theory
of interest. "Money," he declared, "was the creature of law which
gave it the power to represent value, to measure value, and to
accumulate value by interest,"[7] properties which might be given
to any convenient substance. Monetary value did not depend upon
the material of which money was made but rather upon the legal
right to accumulate additional value by interest. The prevailing
interest rate fixed the value of a dollar as a medium of exchange.[8]
Kellogg suggested that the Federal Government should issue a
paper currency through branch offices. This currency was to be

[4] Dewey, *Financial History of the United States*, 348.
[5] Destler, *American Radicalism*, 8.
[6] *Ibid.*, 51.
[7] Edward Kellogg, *Labor and Other Capital*, 42.
[8] *Ibid.*, 56, 58.

loaned to individuals upon real estate security, with a uniform interest rate throughout the nation. This uniformity of interest would secure to labor and capital their respective rights, and this currency, representing actual value on real estate mortgages, would possess a uniform value. To protect against an over-issue of this money, provision could be made to convert it into government bonds at an interest rate slightly lower than that prevailing on mortgages. Thus the currency would have a quality of flexibility —known as interconvertibility—needed to meet changing business conditions. Legal tender powers would complete its qualifications as a medium of exchange. Kellogg believed that the adoption of this theory would destroy the money monopoly and eliminate land speculation and poverty. Debtors would free themselves of debt and a plentiful supply of currency would benefit day laborers as much as property owners.[9]

Labor and Other Capital increased in popularity after 1861 when Edward Kellogg's daughter, Mary Kellogg Putnam, brought out a revised edition. Another revision followed in 1875. Many subsequent monetary reformers gave credit to Kellogg as the source of their ideas. Among them were Alexander Campbell, who published *The True American System of Finance* in 1864, and whose influence in the West lasted for twenty-five years,[10] and Robert Schilling, who referred to Kellogg's book as "the Bible of the early currency reformers."[11]

Labor leaders who accepted Kellogg's theories persuaded the National Labor Union to make monetary reform one of its major objectives in 1867. The National Labor Union's platform called for abolition of the national banks, which had the power to issue money upon the basis of the federal bonds they owned. Instead, the government would become the only agency issuing currency, which it would lend to citizens on the security of a business or property at one percent interest, and which would be convertible into bonds bearing three percent interest. This low interest rate was expected to dissuade capital from investing in government bonds and induce it to invest in industry; this action, it was

[9] *Ibid.*, 250, 280.
[10] Destler, *American Radicalism*, 51, 56.
[11] Robert Schilling, *History of the People's Party, Official Souvenir of the National Convention of the People's Party at St. Louis, Missouri, July 22, 1896*, 6.

thought, would bring a greater amount of business activity and a higher employment.[12]

There was in this platform a measure of inflation which labor had traditionally opposed, but in the period of recession following the Civil War many labor leaders thought that inflation would do the national economy no harm. What meant most to labor, however, was the loan feature of this platform. Government loans at one percent interest would enable labor to secure the necessary funds to set up producers' co-operatives and to free itself from the wage system.

Adoption of this monetary program gradually pushed the National Labor Union toward political activity. Between 1867 and 1870 the opposition of trade unionists was strong enough to prevent any major step in that direction. But the fifth Congress, held at Cincinnati in 1870, brushed aside the objections of die-hard trade unionist delegates and took steps to form a national labor party.

Early in 1872 the first "political" convention of the National Labor Union met at Columbus, Ohio. One hundred delegates from fourteen states attended. They adopted the name "National Labor Reform Party" and a platform which dealt with land, convict labor, co-operatives, the eight-hour day, Chinese exclusion, and monetary reform. But their main business was the nomination of presidential candidates. The time was propitious. The Republican Party had split into two wings—Radicals and Liberals; the Democrats, out of power for fourteen years, were eager to make concessions. A host of politicians who recognized that a nomination by a labor party would increase their chances for a nomination by Liberal Republicans or Democrats descended upon Columbus. Backstage wire-pulling among these prospective candidates was intense. The convention nominated David Davis, of Illinois, associate justice of the Supreme Court, and John Parker, governor of New Jersey, as its candidates.[13]

Davis carried this nomination as a labor endorsement into the Liberal Republican Convention which met in May at Cincinnati. He received ninety-two and one-half votes for the presidential nomination on the first ballot, but his strength soon disintegrated.

---

[12] Destler, *American Radicalism*, 57.
[13] John R. Commons *et al.*, *A Documentary History of American Industrial Society*, IX, 170, 204-206.

Shortly after the Liberal Republican Convention nominated Horace Greeley, Davis withdrew as a candidate on the Labor Reform ticket. The executive committee of the party promptly called a meeting of the Columbus delegates. Thirty-five answered the call. One group, however, immediately retired, announcing that it was "inexpedient at this late date" to make new nominations. At Philadelphia late in August another group joined dissident Democrats who had refused to accept Greeley as their party candidate and named Charles O'Connor, Tammany Hall politician, as Labor Reform candidate for the presidency. O'Connor received fewer than 30,000 votes. Thus Labor's first Greenback political movement temporarily disappeared.[14]

Pennsylvania played a small but growing role in these early Greenback movements. During the period when the Ohio Idea was developing, Henry C. Carey, Philadelphia industrialist, gave the movement his support. Carey sponsored the theory that a managed paper currency joined with a high protective tariff would insure national prosperity.[15] Among Carey's many associates in Pennsylvania were William D. Kelley and Joseph Wharton. Kelley was Carey's chief mouthpiece in Congress, where he earned the nickname "Pig Iron" by his untiring efforts to raise the duties on iron by proposing amendment after amendment to prevailing tariff rates, and where for fourteen terms he reflected Carey's ideas on Greenbacks, money, and specie payments. Joseph Wharton urged on iron and steel manufacturers the use of Greenbacks to create prosperity, although later he was to repent his heresy.[16]

The National Labor Union's movement had little impact upon Pennsylvania. Some old-time labor leaders in the Commonwealth like William H. Sylvis and John Siney urged the interconvertibility philosophy upon Pennsylvania labor. The movement also attracted the support of some younger men like John P. Davis, editor of the *National Labor Tribune;* John P. James, Secretary of the Miners' National Association; and others who were later to become prominent in the Knights of Labor. But Pennsylvania's votes for the Labor Reform candidate in the election of 1872 were scattered and not recorded.

Despite the failure of the Ohio Idea and the National Labor

[14] Frederick E. Haynes, *Third Party Movements Since the Civil War,* 99.
[15] Dorfman, *Economic Mind in American Civilization,* II, 971.
[16] Arnold W. Green, *Henry Charles Carey,* 169-171.

Union's Greenback campaign a third movement developed. As the nationwide depression of 1873 progressed, the farmers of the Upper Mississippi Valley once more turned to Greenbacks as a solution of their economic ills. Among the grievances of the farmers, the worst was that national bank notes were always scarcest when needed most and were plentiful in good times. The national bank notes were secured by deposit of government bonds in the Federal treasury. In boom times, nonbanker holders of bonds liked to sell them to facilitate speculation in projects promising high returns. This sale depressed the value of bonds and made it profitable for banks to buy them; this action increased the volumes of national bank notes in circulation just when deflation was needed to cool speculation. But when depressions came the speculator wanted to sink in the security of government bonds all that he managed to save from the crash. This drove bond prices up, inducing national banks to sell, automatically reducing bank notes in circulation.[17]

Greenback and Reform parties, demanding an increase in the amount of Greenbacks in circulation, appeared throughout the western farm areas. Their unorganized pressure was one of the reasons for Congressional approval of the "Inflation Bill" of 1874 which would have increased the amount of Greenbacks in circulation to $400,000,000. Delegations of conservative capitalists besieged President Grant to veto the measure, which he did on April 24.[18] This veto served to intensify discontent and to stimulate a movement to organize Greenbackism on a national basis. The movement was led by the Indiana State Independent Party, which called for a meeting of all those interested in Greenbacks at Indianapolis in November, 1874.[19] A special invitation was issued to such labor leaders as Cameron; Trevellick; Horace H. Day of New York, a former Vice-President of the National Labor Union; Moses Field, representative of Detroit Labor Unions No. 1 and 2; and Robert Schilling of Milwaukee, president of the Cooper Union.[20]

The Convention assembled with fifty delegates from Indiana, Illinois, New York, New Jersey, Connecticut, Michigan, and

[17] Shannon, *The Farmer's Last Frontier*, 315.
[18] Josephson, *Politicos*, 193.
[19] Haynes, *Third Party Movements*, 106.
[20] Commons, *Documentary History*, IX, 231, 258, 271.

Kentucky, with E. O. Olleman, of Indiana, in the chair. The meeting adopted the name National Independent Party and appointed an executive committee to select a time and place for a National Convention where the party would write a platform and nominate candidates for President and Vice-President. The Committee included E. O. Olleman; James Buchanan, Indiana attorney and publisher; and Thomas C. Durant, a Washington attorney and long-time supporter of Greenbacks.[21]

After a preliminary convention held at Cleveland in March, 1875, which was followed by endorsement from an anti-monopoly meeting held at Cincinnati in September, the Committee called for a National Independent Party convention to be held at Indianapolis in May, 1876.

Meanwhile the 1874-1875 lame-duck session of Congress, dominated by Republicans, passed the Specie Resumption Act, which provided for a reduction in Greenback circulation to $300,000,000 and for the redemption in specie of all Greenbacks presented to the Treasury on and after January 1, 1879. When the Indianapolis meeting convened, indignation over the Specie Resumption Act was spreading rapidly through the western farm country. Two hundred and forty delegates assembled, all but three of them representatives of farm organizations from eighteen states and the District of Columbia. The convention adopted a "Union Program" which was designed to appeal to both farmers and laborers and emphasized a demand for repeal of the Specie Resumption Act as a means of relieving the depression. It nominated Peter Cooper, New York philanthropist, as its presidential candidate, and Senator Newton Booth, of California, as his running mate. When Booth declined, he was replaced by ex-labor leader, ex-general, ex-congressman Samuel F. Cary.[22]

The National Independent Party made little impression in the election of 1876. Attracted by the dramatic conflict between Hayes and Tilden over the future of the South, the electorate gave the Cooper-Cary ticket a mere 82,000 votes.

Pennsylvania played only a small role in the Greenback movement of 1876. After the full impact of the depression of 1873 made itself felt, Greenback sentiment began to grow. Cary's in-

[21] Haynes, *Third Party Movements*, 105.
[22] *Ibid.*, 106, 107, 109, 111.

fluence became apparent among small businessmen; labor chieftains like Siney, Davis, and James increased their agitation and received strong support from the developing leadership among the Knights of Labor in the anthracite regions. A movement to add to the Greenbacks in circulation also developed among Democrats. Most notable leaders of the movement in the party were Francis Wade Hughes of Pottsville, and Victor Piollet of Wysox. Hughes had long been one of Pennsylvania's outstanding Democratic Party leaders. He had been a member of the State Senate from 1843 to 1845, State Attorney General from 1853 to 1855, and state chairman of the Democratic Party in 1862. Credited as the author of the Public School Act of 1854, he was noted as a brilliant trial lawyer, and had an interest in promoting railroad construction and in land reclamation in Pennsylvania and New Jersey.[23] Piollet was a son of Count du Chaumont's land agent in northern Pennsylvania. Before the Civil War he had been a member of the State Assembly; a friend of Buchanan, he had turned down the offer in 1856 to become his private secretary. After the War he had been twice defeated for Congress, in 1864 and 1868, and had lost his bid for the office of State Treasurer in 1875 by 4,000 votes. He had served as a contractor on several canal and railroad projects in the northern counties, and throughout his career he remained an active friend of Congressman Samuel J. Randall. In 1876, he was Master of the State Grange.[24]

In 1874 and 1875 elements favorable to Greenbacks were inclined to look to the Democratic Party to become the champion of a new Greenback movement, and Hughes, in 1875, was able to persuade the State Democratic Party to include a Greenback plank in the platform it adopted at Erie. Accordingly, little interest developed in Pennsylvania in the Greenback movement growing in Cleveland and Indianapolis. But shortly after the State Democratic Party repudiated its Greenback plank at its Lancaster Convention[25] and the National Democratic Party nominated Samuel J. Tilden, a sound money man, a Greenback movement developed.

The first attempt to effect a Greenback political organization occurred at a meeting held in Philadelphia on August 2, 1876,

[23] J. H. Beers, *History of Schuylkill County*, I, 41-43.
[24] Henry C. Bradsby, *History of Bradford County, Pennsylvania*, 1088.
[25] Wellsboro *Agitator*, August 11, 1877; Pottsville *Republican*, October 23, 1885.

at which Edward M. Davis presided and Thomas Phillips served as secretary. Davis was a wealthy Philadelphian, a supporter of many reforms, a former Quaker who was dismissed from the Society of Friends in 1861 for joining General Fremont as an adviser. He was now interested in promoting increased Greenback circulation as a needed economic reform. Others who promised to help the new movement were Francis Hughes, Samuel Mifflin of Columbia, Thomas C. McDowell of Dauphin, and Milo H. Townsend of Beaver. The meeting endorsed the Indianapolis platform. An executive committee was formed to prepare an address to the people and to choose presidential electors.[26] S. L. Youngman, of Philadelphia, became chairman of the executive committee and John M. Davis, editor of *The National Labor Tribune,* was named sub-chairman for western Pennsylvania. In September, the committee issued an "Address to the Voters" and a partial list of presidential electors.[27]

Greenback activity in the state developed in only a few scattered areas. In western Pennsylvania activity was confined to Beaver and Mercer counties and a few wards in Pittsburgh; in the central part of the state it was limited to Lycoming, Northumberland, and Dauphin counties; in the east it centered in Berks, Luzerne, and Schuylkill counties.

Although the campaign in Pennsylvania garnered few votes, it could not be considered a complete failure. Despite Republican pressure and its exhortation that a vote for Peter Cooper was a vote for the opposition, there were areas where a sizeable number of people were willing to vote independently. Cooper polled over 300 votes in each of the following counties: Schuylkill 1,238, Allegheny 769, Lycoming 717, Luzerne 600, Dauphin 397, Berks 333. The remainder of his votes were scattered. Of the 82,640 votes Cooper received in the nation, 7,204 were cast in Pennsylvania.[28] How many Greenback votes were cast and not counted, as Terence V. Powderly charged, is unknown. He maintained that

---

[26] New York *Times,* August 3, 1876. The *Times* expressed the opinion that it was a meeting of former Democrats who hoped to form a third party that would weaken the Republicans.

[27] Philadelphia *Times,* September 11, 1876. Francis Hughes and Henry Carey Baird were the electors-at-large. Baird, a Philadelphia publisher, was a nephew of Henry Carey and a self-styled political economist.

[28] William P. Smull, *Legislative Handbook, 1877,* 289.

there were over 300 members in the Greenback Club in his district, but on election day only three votes were counted there for Cooper:

> It was disclosed to me that it wasn't because of a lack of votes we didn't carry the district, but because being new and inexperienced, we hadn't selected the right kind of counters to sit on the election board. Yes, it is a fact that one of the members of the election board explained to me that on such occasions as an election it was customary for the board to credit as many votes as might be necessary in that district to the Democratic ticket, "it being naturally Democratic" and that there was no sense in throwing good votes away on weak, foolish, unknown, and unnecessary third parties. I began to think some more and make inquiries in other districts. I discovered that the same practice prevailed in many of them and was not confined to one party.[29]

As in other states, Greenbackers also entered congressional candidates in those districts where there was a near-balance between Republicans and Democrats—an effort to secure the support of the party that most feared a loss. In the eighth district, Berks County, C. Shearer received 1,780 Greenback votes to 15,235 for Clymer, the successful Democratic candidate. In the fourteenth district, comprised of Dauphin, Northumberland, and Lebanon counties, where John W. Killinger,[30] the Republican candidate, won easily, Harry C. Deming, the Greenback candidate, received 535 votes. Killinger had been endorsed by the Greenback committee of Northumberland County, where Deming received no votes.[31] In the sixteenth district, comprised of six counties, James F. Davis, the Greenback candidate, received 1,317 votes, all but three of them in Lycoming County. The Republican candidate was successful. There had been some mention in October of Demo-

---

[29] Harry J. Carman, ed., *The Path I Trod, Autobiography of Terence Powderly,* 68.

[30] Killinger was first nominated in September by the Greenbackers of Northumberland County and did not receive the Republican District nomination until October when he let it be known that he was ready to bolt the Republican party and run independently. Philadelphia *Times,* September 23, October 15, 1876.

[31] Deming was publisher of two Greenback newspapers: The Mechanicsburg *Independent Journal,* and the Harrisburg *Evening Journal. Ibid.,* October 20, 1876.

cratic support for Davis but it did not materialize.[32] Some of the disappointment with this result was assuaged by the victory of Hendrick B. Wright of Luzerne, a labor reformer with Greenback views, who won election as a Democrat.

Greenback activity for seats in the state legislature was no greater than for Congress. Candidates for the State Senate were named in only three counties: A. P. Erb, Dauphin County, received 508 votes; J. S. Shattuck, Beaver County, received 417 votes; J. C. White, Mercer County, received 408 votes. Greenback candidates for the Assembly were nominated in three counties: A. C. Baldwin, Beaver County, received 449 votes; H. M. Torbett, Dauphin County, received 405 votes; W. C. Holohan, Clinton County, received 1,091 votes. In addition, four candidates ran for the Assembly on the Greenback ticket in Montgomery County but polled only 32 votes.[33] Legislative candidates withdrew in Montour, Lycoming, and Berks counties.[34]

The depressed economic conditions which had spawned the National Greenback Party in 1876 showed no signs of improving as the year 1877 progressed. Indeed, in many sections of Pennsylvania the labor situation grew worse, and the general price and wage scale continued downward. In the anthracite region conditions were described as "labor idle, crops bountiful, but miners had no means to buy even if potatoes are only 50 cents a bushel."[35] Newspaper reports of strikes among the railroad, iron, and anthracite workers in the state revealed the hardships of the working class. It was not uncommon to read, "The rich are getting richer to make the poor poorer."[36] After the strikes of the summer of 1877, meetings were held in various areas of the state by laboring men, farmers, lawyers, and others interested in forming an independent political party to relieve economic distress.

In Pittsburgh several meetings of working men led by Paul F. Rider, Edward Armstrong, and Daniel A. Fisher were held during July and August, 1877, and at the same time meetings of the Greenback Clubs were held under the leadership of James H.

---

[32] There was a great flush of early Greenback activity in Williamsport, especially after General S. F. Cary spoke there on September 4, but it had tapered off by November.
[33] Smull, *Legislative Handbook, 1877*, 299.
[34] Philadelphia *Times*, October 19, 22, 1876.
[35] Reading *Eagle*, September 20, 1877.
[36] Philadelphia *Times*, September 30, 1877.

Burtt, Albert C. Robinson, and John H. Stevenson.[37] A union of these two groups was made on August 25, 1877, when the Greenback Party of Allegheny County consolidated its efforts with the Workingmen's Party, previously known as the Social Democratic Party, under the name Workingmen's and Greenback Labor Party of Allegheny County. A county convention of this party met on September 8 and selected local candidates and elected delegates to various conventions: two delegates to the Labor convention in Harrisburg, and twenty delegates to the Greenback convention at Williamsport.[38]

Newspaper accounts published in 1877 are vague and indefinite about the groups which attempted the organization of a labor political party in Philadelphia. The newspapers that carried any accounts of the meetings reported the meetings were closed to their reporters. A meeting was held in Calendonian Hall, on August 11, with thirty representatives of trade unions present. A list of resolutions was presented and it was decided to call the party the Protective Labor Party. One of the accounts stated, "A communistic communication from the Workingmen's Party of the United States was offered to the meeting, but it was refused."[39] A committee was appointed to formulate a plan of political organization. This committee met in Philadelphia on August 30 to make plans for a state convention, which it decided to hold in Harrisburg on September 10.[40]

About thirty delegates, most of them from Philadelphia, attended the Labor Party Convention, held on September 10, 1877, at Harrisburg. Presided over by T. W. Spurr, of Philadelphia, the convention adopted a platform and nominated candidates. The preamble to the Labor platform declared:

> The people of this country are in worse bondage than our forefathers were at the time of the Revolution. . . .
> The natural resources of our country are ample for the support of all our people, but through financial mismanage-

[37] A note in the Pittsburgh *Post*, August 10, 1877, stated it was necessary to hold meetings indoors, as the militia stationed in Pittsburgh dispersed outdoor meetings of laboring men.
[38] Pittsburgh *Post*, July 28, August 1, 10, 13, 15, 24, 27, September 10, 1877.
[39] Oil City *Derrick*, August 13, 1877.
[40] Press accounts did not list names of committee members. Philadelphia *Times*, August 31, 1877.

ment and a false and defective system of production and distribution, many of our people are starving and others approaching destitution. The question is whether we shall return into more abject slavery or assert our rights; we ask the people to help us carry out the following principles.

The platform called for shorter hours, protective labor legislation, public education, and Greenbacks.[41] The party made the following nominations: for Supreme Court Justice, Judge William L. Elwell of Columbia County; for Auditor General, John M. Davis of Pittsburgh; for State Treasurer, James L. Wright of Philadelphia.[42]

Response to the Labor platform and candidates was not great. Judge Elwell immediately declined the nomination. Because the western Pennsylvania and anthracite labor leaders were prominent in the plans of the Greenback Party and because Judge Elwell, their strongest candidate, declined his nomination, the Philadelphia labor group decided to join forces with the Greenback Party at its Williamsport convention on September 19, 1877.

Newspaper accounts estimated the number of people present at the first state Greenback convention at from 150 to 400. Thirty-seven counties sent 116 delegates, who selected Francis W. Hughes as chairman, nominated Judge Benjamin S. Bentley of Susque hanna County for Supreme Court Justice, James L. Emerson of Beaver County for Auditor-General, and endorsed James L. Wright of Philadelphia, from the Labor ticket, for State Treasurer.[43]

In many ways the platform adopted at Williamsport was a duplicate of the Labor Party statement. The Philadelphia *Times* commented, "The platform contains much more that is good than could reasonably have been expected and less that is bad than has lately come from any of the side party movements. With the exception of the usual clap-trap about taxing bonds and some

[41] Harrisburg Daily *Patriot,* September 11, 1877; Reading *Eagle,* September 11, 1877.
[42] *Ibid.,* September 18, 1877.
[43] There was some sentiment to endorse John M. Davis but the Pittsburgh delegates would not go along because of the controversy between Davis and Armstrong co-owners of the *National Labor Tribune.* Pittsburgh *Post,* September 20, 1877.

harmless fanciful flights in greenbacks as a universal soothing syrup, there is little to complain of."[44]

The first section of the platform on currency was quite extensive:

> As a remedy for existing evils, a further contraction of the currency should be stopped at once and such currency made a full legal tender. Silver remonetized, and the so-called Resumption act of 1875 repealed. The property of the Federal Bondholders should be taxed as well as that of the farmer, the manufacturer, business man, and mechanic; the whole system of bank note currency should be abolished and gold and silver supplemented by full legal tender paper, except where by terms of contract it is otherwise provided. Legal tender paper receivable for all dues, public and private, and sufficient for the wants of business, should be substituted therefore; and, in order that such legal tender paper should have a uniform value, it should be interconvertible into bonds of the government.

Other planks announced for a protective tariff on goods which the nation had the materials and skills to manufacture, for government subsidy of American steamships, for arbitration of labor disputes, for payment of wages in money rather than in store orders, and for a common school system supplemented by industrial schools. The platform also demanded the amendment of the Homestead laws to make practicable the settlement of the lands by a system of colonization that would enable thousands of families to become self-sustaining, denounced the claims made by the banks for exemption from taxation, and insisted that the government should not pay for a greater interest on its indebtedness than agriculture could afford to pay on its debts.[45]

Greenback political action began to accelerate after the state convention. The *National Labor Tribune* announced that it regarded the Williamsport platform as "unassailable."[46] Greenback clubs mushroomed in Reading,[47] in nearly every town of the West Branch Valley,[48] in Westmoreland County,[49] in Fayette County, in Pottsville and throughout the anthracite region, and in Pittsburgh.

[44] Philadelphia *Times*, September 20, 1877.
[45] Reading *Eagle*, September 20, 1877.
[46] Philadelphia *Times*, September 25, 1877.
[47] Reading *Eagle*, September 25, 1877.
[48] Philadelphia *Times*, September 26, 1877.
[49] *Ibid.*, October 19, 1877.

Frank P. Dewees, of Pottsville, was made state chairman of the Greenback Party at Williamsport. Dewees had been a Democrat who had served several times as county chairman of that party. After the war he had become interested in the manufacture of iron in Kentucky but had returned to Pottsville in 1870. He was an active man and, like his uncle, Francis Hughes, was interested in many projects. An excellent orator and writer, he published a history of the Molly Maguires in 1877.[50] One of his first acts after assuming the state chairmanship of the Greenback Party was to meet with Philadelphia labor leaders on October 4, 1877, in the office of Edward M. Davis, the well known Philadelphia reformer, in order to explore the possibilities of a combined campaign. The conferees decided that the two groups should unite under the name of the United Greenback Labor State Central Committee, which included Dewees as chairman; Frank A. Kauffman of Philadelphia as vice-chairman; Frederick Turner of Philadelphia; Charles N. Brumm of Pottsville; A. C. Robinson of Pittsburgh as secretary; and Uriah S. Stephens of Philadelphia as treasurer.[51] The committee was thus composed of three labor men —Stephens, Kauffman, and Turner—and three Greenbacks— Dewees, Brumm, and Robinson. The committee did little effective work during the campaign. The correspondence of Dewees shows no further communication with the Philadelphia labor leaders and it can be assumed that he received little cooperation from them and managed the campaign without their support.[52] Cooperative organization, in fact, never became a strong point in the Greenback-Labor campaigns. Dewees tried, largely through his own efforts, to perfect a state organization by working with Greenback leaders in each area, but he was continually harassed by a lack of funds in the state campaign headquarters. Each county, area, or city organization seemed to be a unit almost unto itself.[53]

[50] Washington *Post,* November 6, 1899.
[51] Philadelphia *Times,* October 5, 1877.
[52] Frank P. Dewees, "An Address to the People of Pennsylvania," October 15, 1877, carried the names of Dewees, Kauffman, Turner, Brumm, and Robertson as the State Committee of the Greenback-Labor Party. Frank P. Dewees MSS.
[53] Local conventions of the party during September and October nominated candidates for Sheriff, District Attorney, Director of the Poor, Coroner, and County Surveyor. The following counties nominated candidates: Allegheny, Beaver, Blair, Cambria, Crawford, Cumberland, Dauphin, Fayette, Huntingdon, Lawrence, Luzerne, Lycoming, Montgomery, Northampton,

During the course of the campaign there was much discussion of a merger between Greenbackers and Democrats in Pittsburgh, Lycoming, and Luzerne counties, but as a rule in 1877 the Greenbackers disdained joining with the Democrats in an effort to defeat the Republicans. The party received support from several newspapers, including the *National Labor Tribune,* the Mahanoy Valley *Record,* the Tamaqua *Courier,* the Shenandoah *Herald,* the Ashland *Advocate,* the Pottsville *Miners Journal*, and the Mifflintown *Twice-A-Week*.[54] Its chief platform speakers were Francis Hughes in the east and James Emerson in the west. Greenback activity surged during the October campaign. Large meetings of from 1,000 to 4,000 people were reported at Altoona, Johnstown, Oil City, Pottsville, Pittsburgh, and Philadelphia.

Greenback-Labor Party Chairman Dewees in his address to the people of Pennsylvania on October 15, 1877, declared, "In Pennsylvania both of the old parties have yielded to the power of nonproductive capital and have, subservient to it, descended from the position of great exponents of principles to mere factions scrambling for office." He called for the Greenback Labor legions to arm for the battle of November 6, to pay no heed to the siren call of the older parties, since a vote for either of the older party's candidates was a vote for National Banks and the evils for which they stood.[55]

As the election approached, the Greenback leaders were predicting 100,000 votes for their candidates. The Republican and Democratic parties revealed some concern. A. K. McClure, writing in the Philadelphia *Times,* declared, "This united movement of the Greenback men and Labor reformers is likely to prove an important if not a controlling factor in the pending struggle."[56] Newspapers of both major parties appealed to their followers not to wander into the bypaths of the Labor and Greenback movement. "Beware of false gods" was the parrot cry of the average organ.[57]

Perry, Philadelphia, Potter, Venango, Wayne, Washington, and Westmoreland. In one or two counties, notably Cumberland, the candidates withdrew before the election. Philadelphia *Times,* September 12, 20, 21, October 9, 10, 12, 17, 19, 1877.

[54] *Ibid.,* September 25, 29, October 19, 1877; Reading *Eagle,* September 12, 1877.

[55] Philadelphia *Times,* October 16, 1877.

[56] *Ibid.,* September 20, 1877.

[57] *Ibid.,* October 18, 1877.

Greenback candidates received only 52,000 votes, with many sympathizers not voting or voting for the older parties' candidates.[58] Twenty thousand of this total came from the three counties where Greenback-Labor activity was greatest: Lycoming, Luzerne, and Schuylkill. In local elections Lycoming and Schuylkill remained Democratic, but Luzerne elected all of its local Greenback-Labor candidates with a vote greater than the combined Republican and Democratic vote. In a few counties where the Greenback Party combined with the Democratic Party on local candidates, it met with success. In Lawrence County, candidates on a Democratic-Greenback ticket were elected Associate Judge and District Attorney. In Washington County the Democratic-Greenback candidates for District Attorney and County Surveyor were elected. For County offices in Huntingdon and Perry, the Republican plurality was less than the total Greenback-Labor vote. In Montgomery, Northampton, and Venango counties the Democratic plurality was less than the Greenback-Labor vote.[59]

The State election results gave the Democrats victory:[60]

	Republican	Democratic	Greenback-Labor
Supreme Court:	Sterrett, 244,480	Trunkey, 251,000	Bentley, 51,582
State Treasurer:	Hart, 241,816	Noyes, 251,717	Wright, 52,854
Auditor General:	Passmore, 242,288	Schell, 251,256	Emerson, 52,988

Since the Democrats won with pluralities of from 6,000 to 10,000 votes, it was apparent that the Greenback-Labor Party vote had been a determining factor in the election of 1877. The merger of the Greenback supporters and the labor reformers, though not marked by astute political organization, attracted sufficient support from the electorate to mark the Party as a definite threat to the organization of the older parties in Pennsylvania.

Analysis of the 1876 and 1877 election returns provides no definite evidence for determining whether the activity of the Greenback-Labor Party was more injurious to the hopes of the Republicans or to those of the Democrats. Only in Luzerne County, which Greenback-Labor candidates won in 1877, and in which

[58] 200,000 less votes were cast in 1877 than in 1876. Many voters were disfranchised for not paying their voting tax which in Philadelphia was fifty cents. *Ibid.*, November 5, 1877.

[59] *Ibid.*, November 10-16, 1877.

[60] Smull, *Legislative Handbook, 1878*, 324-476.

14,000 fewer Democratic voters and 8,500 fewer Republican votes were cast in 1877 than in 1876, can it be safely said that the Greenback-Labor Party took more votes away from the Democrats than from the Republicans. In other counties in which the Greenbackers cast over 1,000 votes—Allegheny, Blair, Bedford, Dauphin, Lycoming, Philadelphia, and Schuylkill—the Republicans lost a greater number of their 1876 totals than did the Democrats. Two hundred thousand fewer votes were cast in 1877 than in 1876; thus the election of 1877 is perhaps best characterized as one which showed popular disgust in Pennsylvania with Republican control of the national and state administrations. The 52,000 Greenback-Labor votes, cast after the Pennsylvania Democrats dropped the Greenback plank, were protest votes against the organization of the older parties—a united cry for currency and labor reform. This coalition of Greenback supporters and labor reformers made Pennsylvania the leading vote-gathering state for the Greenback Party.[61]

[61] Pennsylvania Greenback-Labor vote exceeded the Greenback votes cast in other states with elections in 1877. The first five in Greenback votes were Pennsylvania 52,852; Iowa 34,228; Ohio 29,401; Wisconsin 26,216; and New York 20,282.

Chapter IV

THE 1878 CONVENTIONS

The increase in Greenback votes in the nation from 82,640 in 1876 to 187,095 in 1877[1] gave leaders of the movement new hope that a re-statement of principles would bring greater success. Greenback and labor leaders, therefore, called a convention to meet at Toledo, Ohio, on February 22, 1878, for the purpose of proclaiming a platform of principles to the nation. The convention recognized Pennsylvania's prominence in the Greenback-Labor movement by electing Francis Hughes as permanent chairman and naming Uriah S. Stephens, Philadelphia tailor, chief organizer in 1869 of Local Assembly Number One, and Grand Master Workman of the nationally organized Knights of Labor, one of the vice-presidents.[2] It was at Toledo that the party adopted the name of National Greenback-Labor Party and issued its famous Union platform.

The preamble of this platform placed the blame for the nation's economic paralysis upon the legislation passed by the Republican and Democratic parties. It stated, further, that the National Greenback-Labor Party had been formed to elect men to office who would pledge themselves to carry out its principles—principles designed to restore economic prosperity. The platform's currency planks called for the suppression of bank-issued currency and demanded that the circulating medium, whether of metal or paper, be issued by the government and made full legal tender for all debts, duties, and taxes in the United States at full value, and that coinage of silver be unlimited. This currency statement represented the feeling that an increase in government-issued currency, either paper or silver, or both, would aid materially the lot of the farmers, workingmen, and small businessmen. In addition the platform demanded a graduated income tax, the donation of public lands to actual settlers, shorter hours of work, and the abolition

[1] Pennsylvania had the largest percentage increase. Its vote increased from 7,204 to 52,988, or to twenty-eight percent of the National Greenback vote cast in 1877.
[2] Dulles, *Labor in America,* 128-130.

of contract and oriental labor. The income tax clause represented the workingmen's feeling that the wealthy should carry more of the tax burden and represented also a protest against the *laissez-faire* philosophy prevalent in the relationship between business and government. The public lands statement was an outright protest against the extensive land grants given to the railroads. Contract labor was a bitter subject with workingmen and this Greenback-Labor platform protested against the practice of corporations contracting for immigrant labor in Europe. All occidental labor in the United States protested Chinese labor in California. The eight-hour day was the workingman's dream. The platform concluded with the hopeful statement that "the adoption by the government of the American monetary system as proposed in the principles of the platform would harmonize all economic differences and settle the differences between capital and labor.[3] It was hoped by the Greenback-Labor leaders that this platform would attract the vast number of dissatisfied farmers and workingmen to the Party's banner in its crusade for political power.

Before the convention adjourned, Frank P. Dewees, chairman of the Pennsylvania Greenback-Labor State Committee, was selected as a member of the National Executive Committee of the party.[4] Upon his return to Pennsylvania, he busied himself preparing for the state convention to be held in May at Philadelphia. His correspondence reveals that he hoped to make the convention harmonious and that to accomplish this he urged all county Greenback-Labor committees and conventions to select their delegates and certify them to him before the convention opened. Dewees realized the importance of harmony among the agriculture, labor, and business groups who comprised the third party in Pennsylvania. He knew that 1878 was the year the party would have to demonstrate its strength and that a harmonious convention would be the first important step toward a successful campaign.[5]

[3] Philadelphia *Times*, February 23, 1878.
[4] Oil City *Derrick*, February 23, 1878.
[5] Lebanon county certified P. H. Reinhardt, J. B. Embick, and W. A. Lockard. Albert Garrett to Frank P. Dewees, March 10, 1878. Frank P. Dewees MSS. Newspaper accounts carried the names of other delegations. Lehigh county delegates were George Fry, Henry Kuntz, Leopold Kern, and I. M. Cassell. Carbon county delegates were Dr. T. E. Davis, E. T. McDonough, Hugh McGarney, William Nutter, and A. Stroh. The Luzerne county delegation consisted of Terence V. Powderly, N. Kiefer, W. G. Thomas, Joseph Powderly, William Harder, F. S. Boyle, and T. M. Carniff. Philadelphia *Times*, April 2, 5, May 6, 1878.

The February, 1878, municipal elections produced three Greenback or Greenback-Labor mayors in Pennsylvania: Terence V. Powderly at Scranton, M. H. McNair at Meadville, and William Barnsdale at Titusville. This action by the voters, coupled with the enthusiastic reports from the spring meetings of the county conventions of the new party, suggested to the leaders of the movement that the election of a Greenback-Labor candidate as Governor of Pennsylvania was within the realm of possibility. Four men were receiving mention for the party's nomination: William H. Armstrong, well known in Lycoming lumber circles; Samuel Mason, lawyer and early advocate of Greenbacks in Mercer and Beaver counties; Hendrick B. Wright, congressman and friend of labor, and Victor E. Piollet, Master of the State Grange. Armstrong and Mason were former Republicans; Wright and Piollet were ex-Democrats. Armstrong, because of his long association with the Republican Party, was suspected by labor of being a Cameron man; he was supported by the lumber interests and Wright of Luzerne was supported by eastern labor.[6] Mason had the support of some western Pennsylvania agriculture and labor delegates and eastern Greenback advocates like Hughes, Dewees, Baird, and E. M. Davis.[7] Piollet hoped for enough support from agricultural delegates to make him a strong contender.[8]

The large number of candidates was significant in that they revealed the varied economic and political philosophies contained within the party. On the one hand was a labor group, led by such men as Thomas Armstrong, publisher of the *National Labor Tribune* in Pittsburgh, organ of the Amalgamated Iron and Steel workers; James L. Wright of Philadelphia, a leader of the Anti-Monopolist movement in Pennsylvania; Uriah Stephens and Terence Powderly, leaders of the Knights of Labor. On the other hand were the currency reformers like Hughes, Dewees, Baird, Davis, William H. Armstrong, Mason and David Kirk. At best the alliance was a strange one. One element was interested pri-

[6] James L. Wright speaks of "lining up" labor delegates in Philadelphia for Hendrick B. Wright as a possible choice for Governor at the Greenback-Labor convention. James L. Wright to Samuel J. Randall, April 28, 1878. Samuel J. Randall MSS.
[7] Wright to Randall, April 27, 1878, Randall MSS.
[8] Victor E. Piollet told Samuel J. Randall that he would accept the Greenback nomination, Victor E. Piollet to Samuel J. Randall, May 5, 1878. Randall MSS.

marily in labor reform; the other group, made up of disgruntled Republicans and Democratic currency reformers, had various ideas on what the Greenback-Labor Party should accomplish. Some thought of it as the new party that would replace one of the older parties, as had the Republican Party in 1856; some hoped to unite the Greenback-Labor Party with one of the older parties or to force either the Republican or Democratic Party to liberalize its views on currency.

This variation in philosophy gave the State Greenback-Labor Party convention which opened in Philadelphia's Concert Hall on May 8, 1878, an appearance of great disharmony. The session opened with a heated and noisy debate over the seating of the Philadelphia labor delegation and over the selection of a temporary chairman. A Greenback delegation with David Steinmetz as chairman had already taken their seats in the Hall when the Philadelphia labor delegation arrived under the leadership of D. J. Kilgore. After a period of confusion over seating this delegation, it was decided to elect a temporary chairman who would then appoint a credentials committee to consider the question of seating the Philadelphia group.[9]

David Kirk, the temporary chairman, was born in Scotland in 1831 and came to Pennsylvania in 1839. One of the early promoters of oil in Pennsylvania, he drilled his first well at Franklin in 1862, and established a refinery and "oil yard" there. By 1870, his refinery was knocked out by freight discriminations and earnings of his life were swept away. As a Greenback candidate for Congress in 1878 and 1880, he lost by narrow margins. After his retirement from the Greenback movement he returned to oil and organized the Pure Oil Company and served as its President.[10]

Kirk appointed a credentials committee with labor sympathizers in the majority[11] to certify delegates and then adjourned the convention until the afternoon. At this session the credentials committee reported in favor of seating the contested labor delegation

[9] Philadelphia *Times*, May 9, 1878.

[10] *Handbook of Petroleum*, I, 669.

[11] Charles N. Brumm of Schuylkill; A. C. Smith of Columbia; I. E. Dean of Venango; T. V. Powderly of Luzerne; Dr. J. A. Killy of Armstrong; William Blakely of Allegheny; Charles Wilson of Dauphin; C. E. Lyman of Clinton; F. W. Hughes of Schuylkill; W. D. McGeary of Clarion; William Caldron of Fayette; W. S. Reck of Westmoreland; Frederick Nevegold of Bucks; E. Philips of Lawrence; and J. E. Emerson of Beaver. Philadelphia *Times*, May 9, 1878.

of Philadelphia headed by Dr. W. C. Crooks, H. C. Baird, H. P. Bender, Thomas Kelley, Charles M. Dupuy, Henry Gioswith, S. P. Chase, James E. Neale, J. A. Solliday and William H. Dewees. Temporary Chairman Kirk then named a committee on permanent organization and a committee on resolutions and adjourned the convention until later in the day.[12]

The evening meeting was opened by Chairman Kirk at eight-thirty when the following list of permanent officers recommended by the Committee on Permanent Organization was elected:

President—Francis W. Hughes, Schuylkill
Vice-Presidents (Listed as to State Senatorial Districts)[13]

1. Philadelphia	John M. Driver
2. Philadelphia	I. W. Bisbing
3. Philadelphia	Frank Bout
4. Philadelphia	Charles M. Dudley
5. Philadelphia	L. Samler
6. Philadelphia	James W. Rayle
7. Philadelphia	Henry Carey Baird
8. Philadelphia	John Devine
9. Delaware	Major Brown
10. Bucks	Robert K. Tomlinson
11. Berks	John Amrein
12. Montgomery	E. M. Davis
13. Lancaster	William Snyder
14. Lancaster	Addison Eby
15. Dauphin	D. S. Early
16. Lehigh	George Fry
17. Lebanon	P. H. Rinehart
18. Northampton	C. P. Comp
20. Luzerne	Nicholas Kiefer

[12] The Committee on permanent organization: Dr. Diffenderfer of Schuylkill; George Fry of Lehigh; Colonel J. R. Embich of Lebanon; Daniel Brown of Delaware; E. M. Davis of Philadelphia and Montgomery counties; William Reardon of Allegheny; John Siney of Schuylkill; J. A. Cake of Lebanon; A. C. Smith of Columbia; J. L. Wright of Philadelphia; W. H. Hines of Luzerne; J. B. White of Bradford and Henry C. Baird of Philadelphia. The Committee on resolutions: J. G. White of Mercer; E. E. Orvis of Columbia; Alexander Patterson of Allegheny; George Van Viet of Clarion; J. E. Emerson of Clarion; William Holt of Centre; E. Buckholtz of Philadelphia; Elmer Smith of Bedford; C. C. North of Huntingdon; W. Sacrioz of Tioga; A. T. Barnes of Cumberland; J. E. Dean of Venango; Thompson Burton of Erie; D. S. Early of Dauphin; D. J. Kilgore of Philadelphia; and W. G. Thomas of Luzerne.
[13] Philadelphia Times, May 10, 1878. The list of men nominated as Vice-Presidents indicated the almost statewide support the Greenback-Labor movement had in Pennsylvania; only five senatorial districts were missing.

21. Luzerne   J. A. Harner
22. Monroe, Pike and Carbon   W. A. Graves
23. Bradford and Wyoming   L. Hanna Smith
24. Sullivan, Columbia, Lycoming
    and Montour   E. S. Watson
25. Tioga, Potter and McKean   Charles Mage
26. Susquehanna and Wayne   G. W. May
27. Union, Snyder and West-
    moreland   John Kelly
29. Schuylkill   J. H. Pomeroy
30. Schuylkill   John Parker
32. Cumberland and Adams   C. E. Goldsborough
33. Franklin and Huntingdon   A. P. White
34. Clinton, Clearfield and Centre   William Holt
35. Blair and Cambria   T. Trefts
37. Indiana and Jefferson   J. R. Bixler
38. Cameron, Elk, Clarion and
    Forest   John Hickey
39. Westmoreland   G. W. Humbaugh
40. Fayette and Green   Levi J. Jefferson
41. Butler and Armstrong   D. J. A. Kelly
42. Allegheny   Gen. William Blakely
43. Allegheny   H. F. Hessey
44. Allegheny   R. A. Hall
45. Allegheny   E. E. Cotton
47. Lawrence and Mercer   J. G. White
48. Warren and Venango   H. P. Kinear
49. Erie   A. J. Foster
50. Crawford   L. W. Wickstone

Secretaries

    John T. Duff   A. C. Silvy
    T. A. Armstrong   H. C. Baird
    Fred Turner

After Francis Hughes was installed as permanent chairman, the convention proceeded to nominate candidates for governor. The nominations clearly reflected the various interests and sections which were attempting to gain prominence in the Greenback movement. William H. Hines of Luzerne nominated Samuel R. Mason.[14] T. A. Hall of Pittsburgh nominated Colonel Tom Marshall of

---

[14] William H. Hines, called "the voice of the laborer" served as a Democratic-Greenback in the House in 1879, and in the Pennsylvania Senate from 1883 to 1886 where he sponsored and supported legislation for the benefit of labor. George B. Culp, *Families of the Wyoming Valley,* II, 613.

Allegheny. A. C. Smith of Columbia made an enthusiastic speech in nominating William H. Armstrong of Lycoming. L. H. Smith of Bradford nominated Victor Piollet. Edward Genane of Bradford nominated William Holt of Centre County, and C. M. Weber of Montgomery nominated George M. Corson of Montgomery.

Mason had considerable support from the oil and agricultural interests of western Pennsylvania. He also had support in the east from men like Hughes, Baird, and Davis and some in the anthracite area as attested by his nomination by Hines of Luzerne County. Armstrong was the candidate of the lumbering section of Pennsylvania. Powderly supported Wright, champion of labor reform in Congress, and this indicated support of the Knights of Labor segment of the party. Piollet hoped for enough agricultural support to be a possible compromise candidate. Marshall, Holt, and Corson had only small local followings.

Nominations for Judge of the Supreme Court followed. Western Pennsylvania delegates named sitting Judge Daniel Agnew of Beaver County. Philadelphia labor nominated Judge Bentley of Lycoming. Nominations were then made for Lieutenant Governor and Secretary of Internal Affairs.

The convention then proceeded to ballot on its candidate for the Supreme Court.[15] Judge Bentley defeated Judge Agnew 114 votes to 94,[16] an action generally regarded as a victory for Philadelphia labor over Pittsburgh labor and its leader, Tom Armstrong. The Philadelphia *Times* commented, "The nomination of Bentley was made by Philadelphia Labor who took sharp advantage to lay Armstrong on the shelf."[17] Personal jealousy, suspicion of Armstrong's Republican sympathies, opposition from Philadelphia Anti-Monopolist and Knights of Labor leaders to Armstrong, a strong craft unionist, seemed to be the basis for this feeling of animosity.

[15] In the Pennsylvania Greenback Convention in this period candidates were always selected before platforms were adopted. This convention started balloting for judge first, as delegates were split over Agnew and Bentley and the eastern delegates hoped to gain an advantage by holding the ballot now before compromises and bargains could be made overnight.

[16] Judge Agnew had been on the court since 1863 and was not renominated by the Republicans. Armstrong, publisher of the *National Labor Tribune,* considered Agnew a friend of the party and the strongest possible candidate they could nominate.

[17] Philadelphia *Times,* May 9, 1878.

The convention next balloted on the candidate for Governor.
S. R. Mason was nominated on the second ballot:

Mason	115
Wright	57
Armstrong	24
Piollet	2

Christopher Shearer[18] was chosen as the candidate for Lieutenant Governor and James L. Wright[19] was chosen as the candidate for Secretary of Internal Affairs.

After the nomination of candidates had been completed, D. Y.
Kilgore, of the committee on resolutions, read the platform, which
represented the philosophies of the fiat and labor reform wings
of the party. The platform blamed the Republican and Democratic
parties for the poverty of the people and for government corrup-
tion, and made the following demands to insure the "prosperity
and progress of a free people": free public lands to be given to
the people, Greenbacks to be issued in sufficient quantity to end
poverty, bonds to be paid according to terms agreed upon, no
new bonds to be issued except for the redemption of those payable
in coin, no tax exemptions to be made except on government
property, corporate combines to be checked by law, tax restrictions on voters to be eliminated, and women to be allowed to
vote, wages to be raised and working hours lowered, and education to be free, secular, and industrial.[20]

These resolutions produced strong objections, and after considerable argument against them from the floor by David Kirk
and A. C. Smith, who regarded them as being too radical, they
were tabled and the convention adjourned until the next day.
This action represented the first serious split in the Pennsylvania
movement. The majority of the delegates at the convention were
conservative currency reformers who wanted a Government-issued
currency regulated by the Government as to credit needs and de-

[18] Christopher Shearer lived in Tuckerton, Berks County. He was a former
building contractor, and a Republican who was opposed to the policy of
contraction. *Ibid.*, May 10, 1878.

[19] Wright had been the Party's nominee for State Treasurer in 1877. He
operated a tailor shop in Philadelphia, and at this time was about fifty-nine
years of age. He stated, "I have acted with the workingmen since I was
nineteen." He was president of the Anti-Monopoly Convention held at
Harrisburg in March, 1876, and temporary chairman of the National Labor
Convention held in Pittsburgh in April of the same year. *Ibid.*

[20] The Philadelphia *Times*, May 10, 1878.

mands. This currency, they felt, should be convertible to government bonds and backed by security as land mortgages. The majority of delegates were men of means, or property holders now financially pressed, who desired an increased flexible paper currency, not an unlimited one.[21]

When the convention re-assembled the next day, May 9, a new set of resolutions was presented by Francis Hughes and adopted by the delegates. The rewritten platform advocated the regulation of currency as "the highest prerogative of government as to volume and value." On government bonds, it spoke only as to payment of them according to the original contract. Nothing specific was mentioned concerning government regulation of business and the free elective franchise statement for men and women contained in Kilgore's resolutions was omitted. The platform asked for a free education system, "to enable labor to avail themselves of a worthy use of leisure." Instead of banks, it asked for a postal depository for the saving funds of workers. The resolutions suggested a public works program under government auspices and also demanded that the state government adhere to the provisions of the new state constitution by ceasing to issue special privileges and charters. A demand was made for legislation that would abolish special rates and rebates on public carriers.[22]

The party adherents supporting the majority platform represented the farmers hurt by low produce prices, oil and lumber interests bothered by depression in their business, small business men who wished for more prosperity, and lawyers and politicians with varying interests. All of these were more interested in a government-issued currency as the solution to the economic depression than in a program of labor reform. Labor reform was not omitted from this platform but references to it and to currency were not as broad or as concrete as in the resolutions read by Kilgore.

The hope of winning the votes of dissatisfied members of the

[21] Samuel R. Mason, for example, was an able lawyer now in financial difficulty. Judgments totalling over $25,000 were entered against him in November, 1878. The Philadelphia *Times,* November 11, 1878. Francis Hughes had overexpanded in his investments in railroad construction and in the project to drain the marsh lands of Long Island and Staten Island. John H. Beers, *History of Schuylkill County,* I, 43.

[22] Francis Hughes and David Kirk were credited with the authorship of this platform. *Ibid.*

old parties also influenced the adoption of this platform. These votes would contribute to a possible Greenback victory in November—if not complete victory, at least the opportunity of holding the balance of power in the State Legislature. It was expected that the additional votes gained from the old parties would offset any loss of votes from the disgruntled fiat and labor wings of the party after the rejection of their resolutions in the party platform.

Before the convention adjourned, Frank Dewees was again made chairman of the State Executive Committee. Word was received shortly before adjournment that Christopher Shearer had declined the nomination for Lieutenant Governor, and shortly after adjournment, that Judge Bentley had declined the nomination for Judge of the Supreme Court. This action by two of the four candidates named by the Convention made it necessary for the Executive Committee to complete the ticket. It met in Harrisburg on May 21 and chose Daniel Agnew of Allegheny County as the Supreme Court candidate. For Lieutenant Governor the committee named Michael Steck of Luzerne County to give their ticket balance, since Mason and Agnew were from the vicinity of Pittsburgh.[23]

To what extent the Cameron Republican machine influenced this convention cannot be accurately determined. Alexander McClure[24] maintained that Mason's place on the ticket had been arranged by Cameron. Certainly Cameron's power was great, and there were some who saw his influential hand in the manipulation of all parties and politics in Pennsylvania. This seems to have been the conviction of Samuel J. Randall's correspondent:

> The political firm of Cameron, Son and Co. after managing the Republican Convention at Harrisburg in the exclusive interest of the re-election of Senator Cameron, surprised the public by repeating the operation at the Philadelphia Greenback-Labor Convention. To its still greater surprise the operation has been repeated a third time at [the State Democratic Convention] Pittsburgh.[25]

[23] During the meeting members reported glowingly on prospects, the fusion with either of the older parties was publicly discountenanced. The evening session at the Court House was addressed by C. N. Brumm of Pottsville, David Kirk of Pittsburgh, John Tomlinson of Altoona, and James Wright of Philadelphia. *Ibid.*, May 22, 1878.
[24] McClure, *Old Time Notes of Pennsylvania*, II, 492.
[25] Brenton Coxe to Samuel J. Randall, May 24, 1878, Randall MSS.

Chapter V

THE 1878 CAMPAIGN IN PENNSYLVANIA

After the May State Convention adjourned, the Greenback leaders showed considerable elation. Reports persisted that a majority of laboring men in Philadelphia and Pittsburgh seemed united for the campaign under their representative leaders: Uriah Stephens, James Wright, and Tom Armstrong. The anthracite region was almost solid in its support of the party, with Terence V. Powderly, Francis Hughes, Frank Dewees, Charles Brumm, and William Hines leading the third-party fight there. The agricultural, oil, and lumber sections of the state had their organizations working for the Greenback cause, with Samuel Calvin, James Emerson, John L. Butler, David Kirk, Samuel Mason, Judge Bentley, and Edward Watson as representative leaders in the campaign. Although opportunists did join the party, there seemed to be no doubt of the sincerity of the majority of the Greenback-Labor leaders in waging a fight for better economic conditions.

Mid-1878 found wages and unemployment of the laboring men, agricultural conditions, and the economy in the oil and lumber section unimproved. A ten-week iron strike in Kensington ended when the employees took a wage reduction. Puddlers were cut from $2.85 per day to $2.40, and helpers from $1.70 to $1.20. Carpet weavers in Philadelphia took a weekly cut of $1.30 on a $10 weekly wage. The Philadelphia *Times,* in August, carried reports from a staff correspondent traveling through the northern-tier counties: "The debtor class embraces two-thirds of the voters of every community. Interest rates on real estate security have gone from 5% and 6% to 10% and 12%." He concluded one survey, "Is it strange that these people want cheap money and they demand it with a vehemence that displays even desperations?"[1]

When the Greenback strategists reviewed the worsened economic situation and considered that the National Greenback Party had polled 52,000 votes in 1877 and that this had changed the

[1] Philadelphia *Times,* August 27, October 23, 1878.

1876 Pennsylvania Republican majority of 18,000 into a Democratic majority of 10,000, they became ecstatic over the effect on Republicans and Democrats if the Greenbacks polled, as they optimistically were expecting to poll, 150,000 votes in November.

Immediately after the May State Convention every Greenback candidate started to campaign. Gubernatorial candidate Mason announced that "he would take the stump right off and keep the ball rolling."[2] Many Greenback club meetings were held and County Conventions began selecting slates in May for the November election.[3] By October forty-three counties had selected slates of candidates for legislative and local offices.[4]

In August Frank Dewees opened the State Greenback Headquarters at the Girard Hotel in Philadelphia. His first assistant was Lee Crandall, Secretary of the State Committee.[5] From Headquarters, Dewees directed the campaign, routed the speakers, listened to complaints, attempted to hold factions together and travelled and spoke in various areas during September and October. The Philadelphia *Times* reported, "His industry and judgment are untiring, and conspicuous, as may be gathered from the amount of work turned out at State Headquarters."[6] He kept all speakers busy. Mason's speaking assignments for one week included: Monday, Shenandoah; Tuesday, Columbia; Wednesday, Wigwam in Philadelphia;[7] Thursday, Sunbury; Friday, Towanda; Saturday, Stroudsburg.[8]

[2] *Ibid.*, May 18, 1878.

[3] It was customary to select county candidates in September and October. A candidate could withdraw or be replaced until election day. Each party printed its own candidate stickers for balloting.

[4] Allegheny, Beaver, Berks, Blair, Bradford, Bucks, Butler, Carbon, Centre, Chester, Clinton, Columbia, Crawford, Cumberland, Dauphin, Elk, Fayette, Forest, Huntingdon, Indiana, Lackawanna, Lancaster, Lawrence, Lebanon, Lehigh, Luzerne, Lycoming, Mercer, Mifflin, Montgomery, Montour, Northampton, Northumberland, Philadelphia, Potter, Schuylkill, Sullivan, Susquehanna, Tioga, Venango, Warren, Washington, Wayne, Westmoreland, and York. Philadelphia *Times*, May 29, October 3, 1878. Not all of these hundreds of Greenback candidates were on the ballot in November. Some withdrew, and in several counties: Bucks, Cumberland, Lancaster, Mifflin and York, little effort was made to wage a campaign.

[5] Crandall had been previously manager of the branch office of the New York *Graphic* and head of the Industrial and Immigration Bureau in Machinery Hall on the Centennial grounds. *Ibid.*, September 23, 1878.

[6] *Ibid.*

[7] Other speakers at the Philadelphia rally on September 25 were Frank Dewees, Uriah Stephens, and Francis Hughes.

[8] Mason was described as a deliberate, analytical speaker, not flowery, or oratorical.

During a visit to Headquarters in September, Mason explained the Greenback Party logic and campaign aims when he answered a reporter's questions:

Reporter: What do you know about Greenbacks?

Mason: Not anything special, except we are working to give you all some if you are entitled to them. But here is some bogus paper money, issued by the hard money people, in which Dewees and I are printed on the face of the counterfeit trash as endorsers. These things are issued by the ton in our country, but the printed sneers at the Greenbackers and the weak jests and flings at "soft" money will tend to help rather than hurt us. There's no fun to be got out of the present stagnation in business affairs and starvation among the laboring classes. If these biting evils can't be remedied by us or through our methods they will never be remedied. In a circuit of eight miles along the Shenango there are twenty-one furnaces and five rolling mills all idle. This involves loss to both the laboring man and to capital.

Reporter: How would you remedy all this?

Mason: Why by stimulating the industries of the country, by getting out enough money into circulation to meet the needs of the people for an ample circulating medium.

Reporter: But tell me, how are you going to get the money out?

Mason: Why, my dear sir, we've thousands and millions worth of bonds which we can redeem. There are about two thousand millions of bonded indebtedness. Now as bonds become due let the government pay them off in greenbacks, and the present holders of these bonds will then lend the greenbacks, at reasonable rates, in the channels of industry. Take for instance the 5-20's. The Government has the option to take them up after five years. Europeans now hold them, or your great bankers, the Drexels; if the Government called them in and paid them off in greenbacks, these gentlemen would turn their money into other investments, probably in industrial, or commercial enterprises, which would of course be a revival of business and a return to prosperity.

Reporter: But hasn't the Government agreed with these bond holders that she will pay them off in gold?

Mason: Yes, she apparently has; but we hold that this pledge was made in bad faith to the people. The contract on the face of the bonds is that they be paid in

the currency of the country, and there is a great
diversity of opinion on this subject. The people who
bought these bonds did so say at the price of fifty cents
on a dollar and they would not be made the actual
losers if they were paid off in greenbacks. My idea is
not inflation but expansion of the circulating medium.
I had a talk with a banker, and he privately suggested,
1,200 millions of paper instead of 600 millions as we
now have. There is no gold out and the national banks
are holding on to all the greenbacks they can get, so
as to prepare for resumption.

Reporter: What about Maine?[9]

Mason: I think Maine is but a foretaste of what is coming this fall, only worse for the old parties. We would
have carried Pennsylvania without Maine, but it is
now put beyond per adventure. We are going to take
votes from both parties. Hoyt is out of question. Mr.
Dewees stated a month ago the contest is between Dill
and me.[10] According to my estimate in the western
counties we are taking from each party in proportion
to their relative strength. All of these western counties
are Republican except Clarion. To sum up, our object
is to concentrate and carry the Legislative ticket and
put an anti-Cameron man in the U. S. Senate.

Reporter: What of Quay?

Mason: Quay's the right man in the right place for the
Cameron party. That act [The Recorder's Bill],[11]
which brought that man down here to Philadelphia
was an outrage. It was done to let him carry this city
in any way he could. I don't see how the people of
this city can endorse Quay's methods, do you?[12]

Mason spoke largely in the eastern counties in the early weeks
of the campaign and finished campaigning in the western counties.
County fairs were favorite spots for speeches from all candidates.

---

[9] Where the Greenback Party in September in fusion with the Democrats
had won a convincing victory for legislative seats. It was the first Republican defeat in Maine since the party's organization. Philadelphia *Times,*
September 9, 10, 1878.

[10] An early optimistic misconception of the Greenback leaders, largely
entertained because the Republicans under Quay did not begin an active
open campaign until late September.

[11] Passed by the Legislature in 1877. It made possible the appointment of
Matthew S. Quay of Beaver County, to the Philadelphia Recorder's office.
Senator Harman Yerkes, Democrat, Bucks County stated, "Percentage of
fees collected in Philadelphia made the Recorder's salary equal to the
President's." Philadelphia *Times,* October 23, 1878.

[12] *Ibid.,* September 23, 1878.

The number of Greenback meetings increased in late October. On October 20, 1878, the following meetings were reported in Philadelphia: Chelton Avenue and Main Streets, Speakers, R. W. Sour and Thomas Phillips; Third and Mifflin Streets, Speaker, Charles S. Keyser; Lancaster Avenue and Aspin Street, Speaker, H. M. Torbett, editor of the Harrisburg *National Standard*.[13] In Pittsburgh more activity was evidenced, with as many as eight meetings reported nightly. Out-of-state speakers were in evidence there; Richard Trevellick of Detroit, James Buchanan and Rev. Gilbert DeLaMatyr of Indianapolis,[14] together with the local orators David Kirk, Tom Armstrong, Colonel Isaac Kline, A. C. Rankin, John Hirsh, William Reardon, Emmett Cotton, George Kennedy, and M. J. Sullivan, made a varied array of talent for presenting the campaign. In addition major speeches were made in various towns and cities by Mason, Hughes, Dewees, Brumm, and Emerson. A concentration of speeches and speakers in Philadelphia and Pittsburgh during the two weeks preceding the election showed a united attempt to win the vote of the workingmen for the Greenback-Labor ticket.

But by the end of October the Greenbackers' early optimism had disappeared. The results of early elections in Ohio, Indiana, and Iowa, where the Greenback-Labor Party had hoped to sweep the elections as they had done in Maine, were far below their expectations and consequently gave rise to a new hope among the leaders of the older parties that in Pennsylvania the Greenback threat was no more real than in Ohio, Indiana, and Iowa. Rumors of Greenback-Labor fusion with the Democrats became prevalent.[15] In late October Samuel Mason had to deny that he was withdrawing as a candidate in favor of Dill.[16] In Pittsburgh, David Kirk, who was waging a vigorous fight for Congress, denied that he was withdrawing in favor of Duff, his Democratic opponent.[17]

[13] *Ibid.*, October 21, 1878.
[14] DeLaMatyr was elected to Congress in October, 1878, from the Seventh Indiana District by a Greenback-Democratic fusion. Pittsburgh *Evening Chronicle,* October 15, 1878.
[15] Alexander K. McClure in his Philadelphia *Times* on October 22, 1878, stated, "Unless common sense prevails in the councils of those opposed to continuance of Cameron domination and a union is formed, it is certain the Republicans will reap the best of the harvest."
[16] Philadelphia *Times,* October 24, 1878.
[17] Pittsburgh Evening *Chronicle,* October 25, 1878.

But in some areas fusion was effected with Democrats and in others with Republicans.[18]

Chairman Dewees' "Party Call to Arms" indicated some of the uncertainty prevalent in Greenback-Labor ranks as the campaign drew to a close:

> As election day approaches your open enemies and secret foes are at work. The air is filled and will be even up to the night of election day with rumors of corrupt bar-bains, defections in your ranks, withdrawal of candidates on the state ticket. Brand all such reports as false and as the machination of the enemy. Mason, Agnew, Steck and Wright are your candidates now and will remain so until the polls close.
> The Republican Party is the representative of ring rule and official corruption. The Democratic is without a policy or fixed principle. Then to attend to duties of voting. Nationals! The tickets are prepared and at the proper time will be placed in reliable hands. Be sure you have a proper and full National Greenback-Labor ballot.[19]

The 1878 Republican State Convention met at Harrisburg. The platform adopted was short. Currency was not mentioned, and the only statement that might have pleased the laborer was, "The public lands should be reserved for actual settlers, so the industrious poor may be encouraged and aided to enter upon and occupy them." The following nominations were made: Governor, Henry M. Hoyt, Luzerne County; Lieutenant Governor, Charles M. Stone, Warren County; Secretary of Internal Affairs, Aaron K. Dunkel, Philadelphia; Judge of the Supreme Court, James P. Sterrett, Allegheny County.[20]

The Republican Party had a task before it. With the Greenback Party threatening to increase its vote, it was necessary for the Republicans, defeated in 1877, to elect their state ticket and to have a sufficient number of Republicans elected to the Legislature to insure Donald Cameron's election to the United States Senate. This was quite an assignment because the feeling against "Cameron rule" in Pennsylvania had not diminished.

[18] Fusion candidates will be noted when election results are presented.
[19] Philadelphia *Times,* October 29, 1878.
[20] Reading *Eagle,* May 17, 1878.

The job of conducting a successful campaign fell to State Chairman Matthew S. Quay, who did not open the Republican drive until late September, but traveled widely in the preceding months conferring with local leaders. During his travels Quay made an intensive study of chances for success. In counties and congressional districts where it seemed certain the Republicans did not have a chance of success against the Democrats as in Lycoming, Luzerne, Schuylkill, and Twentieth Congressional District (Union, Elk, Clearfield, Clinton, Mifflin, Centre) he withheld Republican candidates and had the Republicans support the Greenback candidates. Where the Republicans seemed assured of victory, as in Allegheny County and other Republican strongholds, he labored to prevent the Democrats from supporting Greenback-Labor candidates.

Candidate Hoyt, in September, began his campaign by speaking at county fairs. In October, out-of-state speakers were imported, including Roscoe Conkling, who spoke in Philadelphia; Representative James A. Garfield of Ohio who spoke in Harrisburg, Erie, and Pittsburgh; and Ohio Congressman J. T. Updegroff who spoke in the western counties.[21] Republican campaign logic attempting to refute Greenback economic philosophy was presented by Hoyt in a Philadelphia speech:

> When Nationals talk of paying bonds in greenbacks and talk about the greenbacks being floated in large volume on credit of the nation, the Constitution and laws aside, their first act is a cheat and a fraud, and no plain, practical business man will trust the industrial firm or nation which pays a solemn promise with a cheap promise, and which never proposes a day of actual performance of either. Let currency agitation cease. The Republican party invented the greenbacks and it has redeemed them from legal and financial infamy. It intends that the laborer who receives them Saturday night for a hundred cents will be able to buy on Monday a hundred cents worth of flour.[22]

Not relying on speakers alone, Quay used a variety of means and methods in conducting this campaign. The northern tier counties, whose economy was based on agriculture, lumber, and

[21] Philadelphia *Times*, October 14, 1878.
[22] *Ibid.*, October 6, 1878.

oil, had many Greenback advocates. Many of the individual Granges in this area followed Victor E. Piollet in advocating Greenback currency and in supporting the Party or Democratic-Greenback fusion.[23] In these counties the Republicans had previously had large majorities, but in September when it appeared that the Greenbackers might win two or three congressmen, Quay decided to institute a "bloody shirt" campaign. He reasoned that since this section had been the pioneer in abolition in Pennsylvania, one way to win the voters back to the Republican fold was to rekindle their prejudices against the South.[24]

To combat Greenback currency, he distributed and had Republican newspapers distribute in campaign supplements the comic Greenback notes that featured Mason and Dewees' pictures. Literally millions of these were circulated to ridicule the Greenback idea of an issued currency.[25] To win oil county votes,[26] much publicity was given to the application made to the State Supreme Court by the State Attorney-General's office for an injunction to prevent freight discriminations by the railroads serving the area.[27] In attacking the Democrats directly, Republicans circulated a pamphlet revealing that the Democratic candidate for Governor, Andrew H. Dill, had been a Know-Nothing. This pamphlet was widely circulated in the anthracite region and in the cities where it was thought it would harm Dill the most.[28] A Quay lieutenant, Colonel Robert L. Orr, headed the Pennsylvania Soldiers' League, whose members were constantly reminded that "All future pensions

---

[23] Piollet spoke of the potential force of the Grange and outlined its size in Pennsylvania. In 1878 it comprised 748 subordinate Granges and 32 county or Pomona Granges. It had its own publications, *The Farmer's Friend* with a circulation over 10,000. Victor E. Piollet to Samuel J. Randall, May 12, 1878, Randall MSS.

[24] Philadelphia *Times,* October 2, 1878.

[25] Reading *Eagle,* October 6, 1878.

[26] A survey of the situation stated, "the dissatisfaction in the oil district has been a distinct advantage to the Greenback Party. In the County of Venango, which casts between 7,000 and 8,000 votes, the new party claims to have 3,000 names on its rolls. The new movement is cutting most seriously into the Republican lines. If the Greenbacks can hold 3,000 votes until election day they will sweep the ticket. Between the Greenbacks and Democrats, the prospects of the Republicans getting any members of the Legislature appear gloomy." Philadelphia *Times,* October 7, 1878.

[27] *Ibid.,* October 14, 1878. The application was still pending on election day.

[28] *Ibid.,* October 18, 25, 26, 1878. Dill was born in Maryland and was the son of a Methodist minister. His being a member of the "Know-Nothing" Party was not denied by the Democrats, but they attempted to show that Hoyt had also been a member.

will be denied them if the Democrats are elected."[29] Twenty-eight
prepared columns of speeches by Republicans of national renown
were widely distributed in newspapers through the State. There
was considerable mention in the Democratic press of the amounts
of money Quay and Cameron spent during the campaign.[30] Bargains on fusion were made by both parties, and the Republican
voters accepted the National Greenback-Labor congressional candidates in the Centre and Lehigh county districts and united with
the Greenbackers on Legislative tickets in Lycoming, Centre,
Clinton, and three districts of Schuylkill.[31] In all of these areas
the Democrats previously had had a majority.

As the election approached, Quay began to issue circular letters
with a definite appeal to special segments of the voters. The one
following was addressed to Prominent Citizens of Schuylkill
County. It included election stickers and appealed to them to vote
for Republican candidates:

> There are 3,300 election districts in Pennsylvania and
> there is scarcely one of them in which some Democrat or
> Greenback cannot, by proper effort or persuasion, be
> secured for our State ticket. I wish you to designate some
> person in your precinct specially for this work, selecting
> some one who will be most likely to succeed. Let him
> make it his sole business on election day to secure at
> least one vote for our State ticket. Enclosed are stickers
> for each of the candidates. Before pasting them upon an
> opposition ticket, the name of the opposition candidate
> should be scratched.
>
> Since the Ohio election, the Democratic Party, are to
> a great extent, abandoning the contest upon the State
> ticket and directing their attention to the Legislature.[32]

Another circular letter addressed to "Nationals of Republican
Leaning," appealed to them not to vote for Greenback candidates,

---

[29] *Ibid.*

[30] Newspaper comments on money spent by the Republicans follow: The
Lancaster *New Era,* December 8, 1878, stated Cameron's successful campaign had cost him $75,000. The Pittsburgh *Post,* October 22, reported the
Cameron barrel had been opened in Allegheny to keep the Democrats and
Nationals from forming a union on Legislative candidates. "Republican
managers have just taken $500 out of Mr. Cameron's barrel and put it in
the hands of a small but active ready-money Republicans of Lycoming
county to help along the election of some soft money members of the
Legislature who are expected to vote for Senator Don." Philadelphia *Times,*
October 31, 1878.

[31] *Ibid.,* October 23, 1878.

[32] *Ibid.,* October 30, 1878.

because it would help the Democrats and "defeat your former friends."

> It is possible that at the approaching election you have made up your mind to act with the Greenback-Labor Party and vote the State ticket of that organization. I hold its doctrines to be fallacious and that its projects, if successful, would lead to universal ruin; but the purpose of this letter is not to argue the financial question. The Greenback-Labor ticket cannot succeed in Pennsylvania. The diversion of Republican votes to its support can have no result except to aid the Democrats. The Democratic ticket has at its head a native of Maryland, who spent half of his life there and sympathized with his party in this state in its only half concealed complicity with treason during the war. Its Greenback composition is almost entirely from the worst elements of the Democratic party. If you accomplish anything by voting the Greenback ticket it can only be to defeat your former friends, whose overthrow can in no way minister to the success of your financial theories, and to prostrate the gallant soldiers and loyal men who are upon the Republican ticket at the feet of the dark genius of rebellion. Consider well before you vote. I entreat you to cast your ballot as you did during past years, on the State ticket, at least.[33]

By election day, all the organizational efforts made by Quay and the Republicans combined to make the Republican cause seem the favorite one.

The 1878 Democratic State Convention met at Pittsburgh. Its platform condemned the Republican Party and spoke against decreasing the circulation of legal-tender notes but mentioned nothing definite about increasing the amounts in circulation. The platform stated, "Gold, silver, and United States legal-tender-notes at par therewith are a just basis for paper circulation." The candidates nominated were these: Governor, Andrew H. Dill, Union County; Lieutenant Governor, John Gertig, Crawford County; Secretary of Internal Affairs, J. Simpson Africa, Warren County; Judge of the Supreme Court, Henry F. Ross, Montgomery County.[34]

---

[33] *Ibid.,* November 1, 1878.
[34] Pittsburgh Evening *Chronicle,* May 23, 1878.

Cameron's suspected influence in the Democratic Party and the parties' low state are reflected in the following comments:

> The Democratic Convention in Pittsburgh has been as subservient to the Pennsylvania Railroad as the Republican Convention at Harrisburg a few days ago.[35]
> The ticket nominated yesterday and the platform adopted are as good as could be put forth by the Democracy out of their limited store of eligible men and political principles.[36]

Milton R. Speer of Philadelphia served as State Chairman of the party for the campaign. He worked in close cooperation with United States Senator William A. Wallace, of Clearfield, in running the campaign.

The Democratic leaders were not united. Samuel J. Randall, speaker of the House, was not happy over the influence Senator Wallace exerted on party organization. There is evidence that some of Randall's correspondents considered Wallace too close to the Camerons.[37] Randall was opposed to Dill's candidacy and Dill wrote Randall on April 24, 1878, disavowing any responsibility for the attacks made on Randall in the State Senate. State Chairman Speer wrote several letters to Randall asking Randall to meet him and make peace over Dill's candidacy.[38] This difference was serious, because Randall's correspondence indicates that he had virtually an organization of his own interested in the election of Democratic congressmen. Randall favored fusion where he thought it would defeat the Republicans, while Speer and Wallace hesitated to fuse with the Greenbacks.[39]

The major Democratic campaign tactics included attacks upon Republican extravagance and placed the blame for the depression on seventeen years of Republican rule in state and nation.[40] The

---

[35] Philadelphia *Times,* May 25, 1878.
[36] Philadelphia *Inquirer,* May 23, 1878.
[37] Piollet to Randall, September 17, 1878, Randall MSS.
[38] There is no evidence in the correspondence that Randall was ever very active in supporting Dill. Milton R. Speer to Samuel J. Randall, April 24, May 2, August 21, 1878, Randall MSS.
[39] Some of Randall's political correspondents: James Hopkins of Pittsburgh; W. S. Black of New Castle; V. E. Piollet of Wysox; Lee Coffroth of Somerset; John Trunkey of Franklin; H. B. Wright of Luzerne; W. N. Allen of Titusville; A. G. Curtin and P. G. Meek of Bellefonte. Randall MSS.
[40] Philadelphia *Times,* September 7, 1878.

party's major campaign speakers were Senator Dill,[41] Senator Wallace, Samuel J. Randall, and General George B. McClellan.[42] Democratic campaign speakers had a difficult time speaking on the major issues of the day:

> If they touch on the currency question they offend either the soft or hard money elements of the party. If they complain of Republican maladministration, they are reminded that a Democratic Congress kept the country in a state of suspense and prevented a revival of trade during the whole of the last session. If they refer to the past record of the party, the absurd inconsistency of their course makes them appear ridiculous.[43]

The Democrats spent considerable time and effort in their press mulling over election returns of 1876 and 1877, reviewing the fact that the Greenback vote in 1877 turned a Republican majority in 1876 to a Democratic one in 1877.[44] The thought everywhere in their ranks by October seemed to be why would not an increased Greenback vote in 1878 increase Democratic majorities? They were hesitant about fusing with the Greenbacks, since they foresaw victory without fusion.[45] Where fusion was discussed, as in Allegheny County, difficulties arose as to which candidate, Greenback or Democratic, would withdraw; this resulted in neither candidate's withdrawal.[46] In a few western and northern counties fusion was effected on Legislative candidates, but more often fusion discussions ended without any agreement.[47]

[41] Andrew H. Dill, candidate for Governor, was a State Senator.
[42] General McClellan spoke in Philadelphia on October 26, at Broad and Chestnut Streets to a crowd estimated at 25,000. Philadelphia *Times,* October 28, 1878.
[43] Philadelphia *Times,* October 4, 1878, reprinted from the Philadelphia *Press.* The *Times* called for a campaign with vigorous statements against the Tariff and on money.
[44] *Ibid.,* October 2, 3, 5, 24, 30.
[45] Chairman Speer and Senator Wallace denied reports a Party caucus had been held on October 20 to consider dropping support of Dill, fusing with the Greenbacks and supporting Mason. After denial, Chairman Speer stated, "prospects for success looked more encouraging." The Philadelphia *Times* further stated the fusion report was put on the wires from Harrisburg to the New York *Times* and the New York *Tribune.* The Philadelpia *Times* called it a Quay trick. *Ibid.,* October 24, 1878.
[46] Pittsburgh Evening *Chronicle,* October 16-25. In the October 23 issue the editor stated, "some Democratic Legislative candidates have offered to withdraw in behalf of a union against the Cameron ticket."
[47] When fusion occurred, it will be noted in the chapter on election results.

The Democratic campaign lacked positive leadership. Much of this lack stemmed from the ill feeling between Wallace and Randall, which dated from Wallace's opposition in Congress during 1875-1876, to Randall's elevation to the Speakership of the House.[48] There is some indication that Randall would have agreed, in October, to Dill's withdrawal as a candidate and to the Democratic endorsement of Mason, a former Republican and a suspected friend of Quay and the Republicans, who probably would not have appealed strongly to Democratic voters. Thus, in 1878, the campaign and reforms of the Pennsylvania Greenback-Labor Party became entangled on the Democratic side in a battle between professional politicians of the party. On the Republican side, the Greenbackers had to deal with the well-seasoned political machine of Cameron, Mackay, and Quay. For the Greenback-Labor Party to have run an astutely managed campaign against these forces, strong central leadership was necessary, but instead the Greenback-Labor Party leadership was exercised in various degrees by former Democrats Hughes, Dewees, and Piollet; by former Republicans Mason and Thomas Armstrong; by labor leaders Powderly, James Wright, and Uriah Stephens, with advice from currency philosophers Baird and Davis. The enthusiasm and the opportunity for success were present for Pennsylvania Greenbackers, but the ineffectiveness of the campaign and of the election results caused many Greenback-Labor supporters to start dropping out of the movement after the election.

[48] McClure, *Old Time Notes*, 394.

CHAPTER VI

THE 1878 ELECTION IN PENNSYLVANIA

In the campaign of 1878, when for the first time it was able to make a concerted effort on a national scale, the Greenback-Labor Party won remarkable success by polling 1,060,000 votes. It failed by only a narrow margin to realize its hopes of capturing the balance of power in Congress. In many sections of the West the Greenback Party drew strength from the Republicans and thus helped to make possible a sweeping congressional victory for the Democrats.[1] Fourteen Greenback-Labor candidates were elected: three from Pennsylvania, two each from Iowa, Illinois, and Maine, and one each from Indiana, Missouri, Texas, North Carolina, and Alabama.[2] Pennsylvania ranked third in the nation among the states contributing most heavily to the increased Greenback-Labor vote in 1878, and it ranked first among the states with a straight Greenback-Labor vote: Iowa, 125,087 (in combination with the Democratic Party); Massachusetts, 109,435 (in combination with the Democratic Party); Pennsylvania, 81,758; New York, 75,133; Michigan, 73,313; Missouri, 61,167; Illinois, 60,-439; Maine, 41,404; and California, 20,752.[3]

In Pennsylvania the election resulted in a complete victory for the Republicans for all state offices, and they maintained their majorities in the Congressional delegation and the State Legislature. The totals for state offices were as follows:[4]

	Republican	Democrat	Greenback
Governor	Hoyt, 319,567	Dill, 297,060	Mason, 81,738
Lieutenant Governor	Stone, 319,003	Fertig, 295,753	Steck, 74,082

[1] Josephson, *Politicos*, 265.
[2] Haynes, *Third Party Movements*, 124, 134.
[3] *The Tribune Almanac, 1879*, 57-113.
[4] Philadelphia *Times*, November 15, 1878. Hoyt had a plurality of 22,000 in the State and a 17,000 majority in Philadelphia. A combination of Democratic and Greenback votes would have insured victory by approximately 60,000.

| Secretary of Internal Affairs | Dunkel, 311,042 | Africa, 301,034 | Wright, 81,733 |
| Judge of Supreme Court | Sterrett, 311,042 | Ross, 287,221 | Agnew,[5] 99,316 |

The Greenback-Labor Party in Pennsylvania did well in its quest for legislative seats. For Congress, the National Greenback-Labor Party had candidates in all but three districts.[6] In Philadelphia the party supported the incumbents in the Third and Fourth Districts, Samuel J. Randall, Democrat, and William D. Kelley, Republican, who were re-elected. Kelley is listed as a Greenback-Republican in some accounts which credit the Greenback Party of Pennsylvania with electing three members to Congress.[7]

In the Congressional districts outside Philadelphia two Congressmen were elected on a fusion basis: Hendrick B. Wright on a Greenback-Democratic fusion in the Twelfth District (Lackawanna and part of Luzerne);[8] and Seth H. Yocum as a Greenback-Republican candidate in the Twelfth District (Centre, Clearfield, Clinton, Elk, Mifflin, and Union counties).[9] The Republicans in this district did not present a candidate, and in this nominally Democratic district Yocum was able to defeat Andrew G. Curtin

[5] Daniel Agnew, Beaver County, who led the Greenback ticket, was a Republican Judge in the Court from 1863. He had been replaced by Sterrett on the Republican ballot. In October he published an address "To the People of Pennsylvania," attacking Quay and Cameron. Pittsburgh Evening Chronicle, October 25, 1878.

[6] Philadelphia Times, November 18, 1878. For a complete list see Smull, Legislative Handbook, 1879, 470-476.

[7] Tribune Almanac, 1879, 53; Haynes, Third Party Movements, 134.

[8] "The Nationals swallowed the Democrats in the Twelfth District by endorsing Wright," Scranton Times, September 23, 1878. But after the election, "Wright recovered his speech to say that he is a Democrat and that the Greenbackers have no right to count him in their party. Colonel Wright knows when to keep still a great deal better than has been supposed. The most powerful kind of mustard plaster could not have drawn such a confession from him before the election." Philadelphia Times, December 6, 1878.

[9] Seth H. Yocum, 1834-1895, had a varied career. Born in Catawissa, Pennsylvania, he learned the printer's trade in Philadelphia, was graduated from Dickinson College in 1860, served in the Civil War, was admitted to the Schuylkill County Bar in 1865, practiced in Ashland and came to Bellefonte in 1873, served as District Attorney of Centre County 1875-1879. He served in the 46th Congress but was not a candidate for re-election. He moved to Johnson City, Tennessee, and became mayor in 1886. Next he was an orange grower in California and died at Santa Moncia. Biographical Directory of the American Congress, 2052.

by 73 votes despite appeals from Samuel Randall to Peter Meek to support Curtin.[10]

There were several Congressional Districts where Greenback-Democratic totals were greater than those of Republican candidates: Fourteenth (Dauphin, Lebanon, Northumberland); Sixteenth (Tioga, Potter, McKean, Cameron, Lycoming, Sullivan); Twenty-second (Allegheny); Twenty-fourth (Washington, Beaver, Lawrence); Twenty-fifth (Indiana, Clarion, Armstrong, Jefferson, Forest); Twenty-sixth (Butler, Mercer, Crawford); and Twenty-seventh (Erie, Warren, Venango). The Pennsylvania twenty-seven-member delegation to Congress comprised sixteen Republicans (with election majorities in only nine districts), eight Democrats, and the three fusion candidates, Wright, Yocum, and Kelley.

The differences in strategy on fusion between Randall and the Democratic organization headed by Speer can be seen in the twenty-fourth and twenty-sixth Congressional Districts. Randall, in these districts, was willing to support a Greenback candidate because he thought he could defeat the Republican, but the Democratic organization presented a regular candidate. From the Twenty-fourth District, W. S. Black of New Castle informed Randall, "Butler County held out on endorsing Emerson (Greenback) for Congress, insisted in putting up Clendenin who will lose. I blame Quay's influence on certain Democrats in Butler County." The vote in this district was Shellenbarger, R., 11,261; Clendenin, D., 10,025; Emerson, G.B., 1,901. From the Twenty-sixth District, W. N. Allen of Titusville had the same information, "I did what I could toward bringing about a union of the Democrats and Nationals. . . . Plummer carried this county. Plummer and his family are destitute. Can you find work for

---

[10] Andrew G. Curtin asked Randall to use his influence in having Peter Meek of Bellefonte support him. Meek replied to Randall he would not support Curtin until he would make certain pledges, "that will bind him, to some extent to the interest of the people. . . ." Andrew J. Curtin to Samuel J. Randall, October 17, 1878. Peter Meek to Samuel J. Randall, October 18, 1878. Randall MSS. The campaign to defeat Curtin was bitter. A. K. McClure stated in an editorial, "It is probable that fraud was invoked to defeat Curtin as the debauchery of the Democratic leaders like Meek and others by Cameron, wouldn't be likely to pause at any fraud that promised the result they were hired to accomplish." Philadelphia *Times*, November 16, 1878.

him in the house. . . ."[11] The vote in this district was Dick, R., 13,821; Plummer, G.B., 12,432; Baird, D., 6,516.

Elections for the State Senate were held in twenty-six districts. Greenback candidates campaigned in twenty-five of them. The Democrats and Greenbacks joined in the following: in the twenty-sixth (Susquehanna and Wayne), where W. H. Nelson[12] won by 560 votes; in the thirty-sixth (Somerset, Bedford, Fulton), where Frederick Groff[13] won by 620 votes; in the forty-second (Allegheny), where J. P. Smith lost by 165 votes; and in the forty-fourth (Allegheny), where Charles Paulson[14] won by 236 votes. There were two Greenback-Republican candidates: John Nyce, in the twenty-second (Monroe, Pike, Carbon), who lost by 4,000 votes, and S. Brooks Caldwell, in the thirty-fourth (Clinton, Centre, Clearfield), who lost by 605 votes. John Parker, Schuylkill County, was the one Greenback candidate elected. The Republicans did not present a candidate in his district.[15]

Greenback or Greenback fusion candidates for the State Assembly campaigned in all but a few of the districts. Seventeen Greenback or Greenback fusion candidates were successful: Crawford, N. L. Thickstan; Fayette, Charles S. Seaton; Huntingdon, B. R. Foust and M. P. Doyle; Luzerne, W. H. Hines, Dennis O'Lenihan, and Thomas Mooney; Lycoming, John Gaus and Peter Reeder; Potter, William Shear; Schuylkill, Patrick Conroy, John T. Shoener, John F. Welsh; Susquehanna, J. W. Cargill, J. C. Morris; Warren, J. B. White; Venango, J. L. Dewoody.[16]

[11] W. S. Black to Samuel J. Randall, October 7, 1878. W. N. Allen to Samuel J. Randall, November 8, 1878, Randall MSS.

[12] W. H. Nelson was from Equinunk, Wayne County. He formerly served in the House as a Democrat. He was a merchant and preacher in the M.E. Church. Smull, *Legislative Handbook, 1879*, 666.

[13] Frederick Groff, Somerset County, educated at Millersville Normal School. Formerly a miller, after 1871 a teacher, school director, councilman, and Chief Burgess of Stoystown. Twice elected Justice of the Peace. *Ibid.*, 663.

[14] Charles Paulson, born in Wilmington, Delaware, where he learned the hat business. He engaged in the hat and fur business in Pittsburgh but died before his term ended. *Ibid.*, 666.

[15] John Parker was born in England but came to America in his youth. He was a blacksmith by trade and at the time of his election was editor of *Parker's Tri-Weekly*, published in Mahanoy City. *Ibid.*, 666.

[16] Shoener, Gaus, Reeder, Seaton, Foust, and Doyle had Republican support. Morris, Cargill, White, Dewoody, Shear, and Thickstan had Democratic support, while Hines, D'lenihan, Conroy, Welsh, and Mooney were straight Greenback candidates defeating both Republican and Democratic candidates in their districts. *Ibid.*, 487-503; 669-693.

The following Greenback-Labor candidates were elected as county officials in 1878: Cameron, Thomas Dougherty, commissioner; Columbia, Alexander B. Herring, commissioner; Crawford, James Jamison, commissioner, William Nash, treasurer, and A. W. Smith, auditor; Forest, F. C. Lacey, auditor; Huntingdon, John Logan, James Davis, and Eli Plummer, auditors; Lycoming, N. R. Keys, treasurer, and William Eves, coroner; Schuylkill, Samuel Garrett, commissioner; Warren, James Ray and W. H. Multiby, commissioners.[17]

1878 County Vote for Governor[18]

County	Hoyt, R.	Dill, D.	Mason, G.	Greenback-Labor Percentage of Vote
Adams	2,742	3,361	139	2.2
Allegheny	20,601	13,186	7,724	18.2
Armstrong	3,007	2,693	1,899	25.0
Beaver	3,571	2,968	436	6.2
Bedford	3,014	3,347	202	3.1
Berks	6,506	13,480	1,755	8.1
Blair	3,700	3,390	968	13.0
Bradford	6,010	3,132	1,846	20.0
Bucks	7,552	7,601	200	1.4
Butler	3,892	3,766	2,216	22.4
Cambria	2,196	3,342	1,081	16.3
Cameron	406	381	219	20.7
Carbon	2,150	2,260	1,041	19.1
Centre	2,059	3,827	1,466	20.0
Chester	8,178	5,466	205	1.4
Clarion	2,265	4,032	1,482	19.2
Clearfield	1,602	3,207	1,198	20.0
Clinton	1,814	2,699	347	7.0
Columbia	1,451	3,278	1,159	19.5
Crawford	5,957	3,833	3,528	36.0
Cumberland	3,743	4,831	556	6.0
Dauphin	6,591	5,320	1,468	12.0
Delaware	4,769	3,137	364	4.4
Elk	426	1,100	378	20.0
Erie	6,044	4,237	1,625	14.0
Fayette	2,654	4,211	1,937	22.0
Forest	318	267	277	32.2
Franklin	4,734	4,691	41	.5
Fulton	794	1,222	—	—
Greene	1,606	3,229	120	2.3
Huntingdon	3,073	2,736	639	9.8
Indiana	3,486	1,557	2,155	30.0
Jefferson	1,944	2,140	814	18.0

(*Continued*)

[17] *Ibid.*, 253.
[18] Lane, the Prohibition candidate for governor, received 3,653 votes. Philadelphia *Times*, November 15, 1878.

1878 County Vote for Covernor (Continued)

County	Hoyt, R.	Dill, D.	Mason, G.	Greenback-Labor Percentage of Vote
Juniata	1,473	1,851	142	4.3
Lackawanna	4,898	1,974	3,588	35.5
Lancaster	15,518	8,714	225	1.6
Lawrence	2,876	1,605	3,093	40.0
Lebanon	3,914	2,646	382	5.8
Lehigh	4,975	6,705	270	2.3
Luzerne	7,322	4,414	6,080	34.1
Lycoming	3,207	4,809	2,062	20.5
McKean	1,504	1,882	742	18.0
Mercer	4,436	3,708	1,850	18.6
Mifflin	1,744	1,756	59	1.8
Monroe	602	2,829	400	10.4
Montgomery	9,006	9,164	381	2.1
Montour	772	1,378	483	18,1
Northampton	4,035	7,501	1,079	8.0
Northumberland	3,281	4,584	1,489	16.0
Perry	2,697	2,711	97	2.0
Philadelphia	70,099	53,755	3,211	2.5
Pike	497	1,135	56	3.0
Potter	1,326	694	669	25.0
Schuylkill	5,994	7,657	6,508	32.3
Snyder	1,814	1,494	154	4.5
Somerset	3,134	2,140	398	7.0
Sullivan	436	602	379	26.8
Susquehanna	3,832	2,216	1,825	23.2
Tioga	4,253	2,128	1,681	20.8
Union	1,836	1,656	172	4.8
Venango	3,482	3,035	1,229	16.0
Warren	2,175	1,026	1,822	36.0
Washington	5,263	4,994	822	7.5
Wayne	1,937	1,625	1,384	29.7
Westmoreland	4,795	5,968	1,642	13.0
Wyoming	1,417	1,600	474	14.0
York	5,960	9,644	79	.6
Total	319,567	297,060	81,758	11.6

Analysis of the tabulation of the vote for governor in 1878 reveals certain interesting facts. The combined Greenback-Labor and Democratic votes exceeded the Republican vote by 60,000. Republican and Democratic candidates each carried thirty-three counties, with the Greenback candidate winning in Lawrence County. In the 1877 election the Democrats won by carrying thirty-seven counties, while the Republicans carried twenty-nine counties and the Greenback-Labor Party won an overwhelming victory in Luzerne. The Democrats would have been able to carry the four counties they lost in 1878 if they had been able to secure the Greenback vote in these counties; but their majority would not have been large enough to win the state election. The Republicans piled up a lead of 30,563 votes in three counties—Allegheny, Lancaster, and Philadelphia—a majority sufficient to compensate for the closely contested elections in the other sixty-four counties.

It is apparent that the Greenback-Labor Party held the balance of power in this election; however, it seems to have been stronger in counties carried by the Republicans than in the counties won by the Democrats. In the thirty-three counties won by the Republicans, the Greenback-Labor vote totalled approximately 49,000; in the thirty-three counties won by the Democrats, the Greenback-Labor vote was only 29,000.

Why the Greenbackers and Democrats did not join forces and end Republican domination of Pennsylvania politics is a question that may never be answered satisfactorily. Statewide fusion was not necessary to win the election for the Democrats. If the Democrats and Greenbackers had united in only six of the strong Greenback-Labor counties—Indiana, Lawrence, Lackawanna, Luzerne, Schuylkill, and Warren—they would have garnered 23,236 Greenback-Labor votes—enough to balance the majority of less than 22,000 held by the Republicans. Why, then, was a limited fusion not effected? Did the Republicans forestall attempts at fusion? Did Democratic leadership oppose union with the Greenbackers? Or did the Greenback leaders perhaps foresee the rise of a powerful new party to replace one of the old parties?

Contemporaneous opinion on the subject is diverse, offering no final answer to these questions. Alexander McClure in his *Old Time Notes,* published twenty-seven years after the election, commented as follows: "Mackay and Quay had the Greenbackers ticketed through with baggage checked with all the Greenback leaders involved in the deal, including the Greenback nominee for Governor, sworn to resist fusion under any and all circumstanes."[19] But contemporary accounts in the Philadelphia *Times,* of which Alexander McClure was editor, stress the fact that it was the Democratic leaders who refused to pursue attempts at fusion. The following editorial, written the day after the election, seems to attribute the fact that fusion did not materialize to the ineptitude

[19] McClure, *Old Time Notes,* 492.

of the Greenback and Democratic leaders rather than to efforts of Republican leaders to prevent a jointure:

> After all shall have been said that can be said about Republican frauds, the fact will remain that the victory is the fairly expressed judgment of the people of Pennsylvania. The political power of Philadelphia and the agencies of fraud which were made available in the end, made up half or more of the majority in city, and the commercial elements in Lackawanna and Luzerne were controlled for Hoyt by means which can't be counteracted but the skillful and powerful in politics as in war are successful because they win success, and that is what the Republican leaders have done. The organization of the Democracy was disjointed and inefficient to a degree that made it a burlesque when compared to the consummate skill and vigilence and desperation which directed the Cameron forces. There is a majority of many thousands against the leaders who triumphed yesterday—more than enough to have carried the legislature by a large majority, but the average political idiots held high carnival in both Democratic and National councils, and the level-headed Cameron has quietly carried off the prize while his divided foes were wrangling as to which of them should possess it.[20]

Preventing a fusion of Democrats and Greenbackers was definitely to the best interests of the Republicans, and they doubtless took steps to forestall such an eventuality. There were other forces, however, which worked to prevent a jointure. One of these was the complexion of the Greenback-Labor Party. Many former Republicans and Democrats were in the party, and each group refused fusion that would benefit its former political enemies.

Another circumstance that tended to preclude fusion was the large number of reformers, disgruntled farmers, and workingmen in the party who, at this time, had no more faith in the policies of the Democratic Party than in those of the Republicans. There were also many in 1878 who saw in the Greenback-Labor Party the future great reform party in Pennsylvania and the nation. Thus a number of forces were at work to keep the Democrats and Greenbackers from joining forces effectively in Pennsylvania.

The map on the following page shows the geographic distribu-

---

[20] Philadelphia *Times,* November 6, 1878.

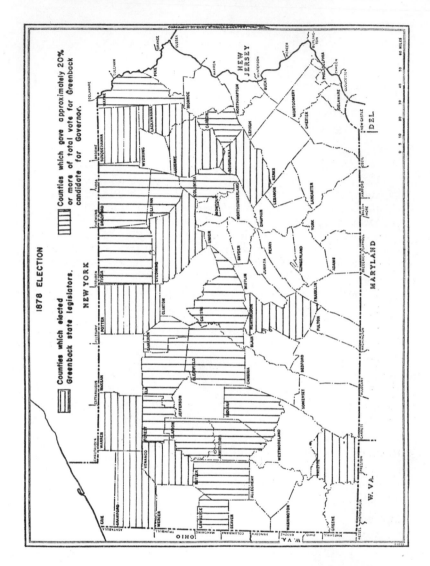

tion of Greenback-Labor Party strength in the election of 1878. Twenty-six counties evidenced strong Greenback support; practically all of these counties were in the northern half of the state. The southern half of the state revealed little real interest in the philosophies of the Greenback-Labor Party. Economic conditions in the northern counties accounted for the interest in Greenback-

Labor principles in this region. During the Civil War period of high grain prices and high land prices, the northern agricultural counties, both eastern and western, had expanded. Depressed prices and high debt charges, in addition to the discovery that their land was better adapted to cattle raising and dairying than to grain farming, prompted many farmers of the area to embrace the principle of the Greenbackers.

In the oil counties, monopoly practices of the railroads and of the Standard Oil Company prompted many to support the reform of the Greenback-Labor Party. In the bituminous and anthracite coal counties, economic conditions were so depressed that the majority of those miners who voted gave their support to the Greenback-Labor Party.

In order to make possible a more detailed analysis of Greenback-Labor Party strength, and to complete interpretation of the results of the election of 1878, the votes in the election districts of three counties are presented below.

In eastern Pennsylvania, Schuylkill County was selected. Schuylkill was then, as it is now, largely a mining area, but a considerable portion of it was agricultural. In election districts whose economy was based upon mining, such as Cass, Frackville, Girardville, Gilberton, Mahanoy City, and Shenandoah, the majority of the votes were cast for the Greenback candidate for Governor. In areas that were predominantly commercial and/or agricultural, such as Hegins, Orwigsburg, Pine Grove, Pottsville, and Schuylkill Haven, the Greenback-Labor Party received little support. Thus Schuylkill County supports most graphically the contention that the Greenback-Labor Party was the party of hope for the destitute and unemployed—in this case, the anthracite miners.

The Centre County table is presented as representation of Central Pennsylvania. The table reveals that the Greenback-Labor vote led the ticket in Boggs, Burnside, Half Moon, Huston, Milesburg, Patton, and Snow Shoe Townships, where agricultural land was poor and much of the economy depended on mining of coal and iron ore. In the areas with better agricultural land, such as Ferguson, Harris, Penn, and Potter Townships, the party ran a poor third. In College Township, the seat of The Pennsylvania State College, there were more Greenback-Labor voters than

1878 Vote for Governor
Schuylkill County[21]

Election Districts	Republican	Democrat	Greenback
Ashland	231	333	436
Auburn	80	49	—
Barry	71	105	6
Butler	81	98	413
Brunswig	137	329	23
Blythe	21	86	70
Branch	94	34	41
Cass	67	147	311
Cressona	99	116	62
Eldred	131	65	11
Frailey	74	20	130
Foster	19	24	61
Frackville	59	74	143
Girardville	88	57	326
Gilberton	55	86	331
Hegins	72	134	27
Hubley	34	65	10
Kline	9	12	190
Landingville	38	65	2
Mt. Carbon	5	41	1
Manheim	85	293	24
Mahoney City	504	406	1,251
Minersville	268	236	112
Middleport	22	18	6
New Castle	71	37	178
Norwegian	48	137	156
New Philadelphia	9	35	23
New Ringgold	22	16	—
Orwigsburg	66	99	6
Pine Grove	201	318	74
Palo Alto	67	126	40
Port Clinton	35	61	7
Port Carbon	189	80	70
Porter	151	74	122
Pottsville	1,091	813	359
Rahn	50	79	120
Rush	59	121	17
Reilly	35	42	150
Ryan	26	57	10
Schuylkill Haven	348	318	17
St. Clair	324	197	228
Shenandoah	180	381	581
Tamaqua	191	341	181
Tremont	162	187	91
Other Townships	481	1,242	65
	5,994	7,657	6,508

Democratic, with one-third of the total votes cast for Governor being for the Greenback candidate.

[21] Smull, *Legislative Handbook, 1879,* 443.

1878 VOTE FOR GOVERNOR

CENTRE COUNTY[22]

Election Districts	Republican	Democrat	Greenback
Bellefonte	279	240	108
Milesburg	36	30	66
Unionville	32	32	13
Howard	36	49	15
Philipsburg	175	144	23
Benner	36	160	44
Boggs	72	163	171
Burnside	18	22	29
Curtin	12	52	27
College	113	74	92
Ferguson	121	225	43
Gregg	60	276	2
Half Moon	38	39	67
Haines	104	207	4
Harris	80	121	7
Howard Township	56	86	32
Huston	40	51	71
Liberty	95	57	33
Marion	33	92	12
Miles	45	246	29
Patton	31	41	75
Penn	37	288	—
Potter	134	377	22
Rush	27	100	70
Snow Shoe	31	75	107
Spring	137	191	111
Taylor	39	48	30
Union	50	69	64
Walker	55	202	59
Worth	37	70	40
	2,059	3,827	1,466

Warren County was chosen to represent the northern counties. The table shows that the party led the ticket in areas that were largely dependent on lumbering, tanneries, and some agriculture, such as Youngsville, Columbus Township, Elk, Eldred, Glade, Brokenstraw, Kinzua, Mead, Pleasant, and Sheffield. The party made a strong showing in Warren Borough and North Warren, or Conewango Township, where oil prosperity was an important factor. In the Farmington area, with its prosperous dairy farming, the party made a poor showing.

Despite the strenuous efforts of the Republican and Democratic leaders in their press and through their political speeches to

[22] Smull, *Legislative Handbook, 1879*, 345.

1878 Vote for Governor

Warren County[28]

Election Districts	Republican	Democrat	Greenback
Warren	184	153	182
Youngsville	57	24	66
Columbus	44	31	26
Columbus Township	66	18	158
Tidioute	148	120	17
Brokenstraw	55	70	81
Conewango	108	74	78
Corydon	30	23	20
Cherry Grove	23	1	—
Deerfield	55	23	21
Elk	35	9	65
Eldred	47	7	66
Freehold	190	24	90
Farmington	187	44	39
Glade	36	21	185
Kinzua	27	10	33
Limestone	34	60	22
Mead	33	26	45
Pine Grove	131	16	128
Pleasant	3	24	31
Pittsfield	118	35	60
Sugar Grove	220	30	169
Spring Creek	105	14	87
Sheffield	47	36	90
South West	91	32	11
Triumph	101	101	52
	2,175	1,026	1,822

mitigate the influence and the policies of the Greenback-Labor Movement, the party made a most threatening challenge to their leadership in 1878. Never again in over a quarter of a century was their leadership of the State so endangered. The 1878 returns show that in six counties—Forest, Indiana, Lackawanna, Lawrence, Luzerne, and Warren—the Greenback-Labor vote was large enough to lead both parties, or at least to be in second place. The location of these counties in Pennsylvania focuses the economic plight of the citizens from these regions and spotlights the elements from which the Greenback-Labor Party drew its strongest support: the anthracite and bituminous miners, and the farmers of the northern counties.

[28] Smull, *Legislative Handbook, 1879*, 455.

CHAPTER VII

1879. PENNSYLVANIA
GREENBACKISM BEGINS ITS DECLINE

The year 1879 opened with the attention of the Greenback followers in Pennsylvania turned to the legislature, where the nineteen newly-elected Greenback members were attempting to make their presence felt. After the Legislature convened on January 7, 1879, they became involved in the House speakership contest. Martin P. Doyle, the United Brethren minister from Huntingdon County, was placed in nomination against the Republican and Democratic caucus choices. Doyle, however, received only eleven votes, when five of the newly-elected Greenback members voted for the Republican choice, and the other voted Democratic.[1] In the Senate, Greenbacker John Parker voted Republican, and W. N. Nelson voted Democratic for President *pro tem.*[2] On February 22, 1879, Donald Cameron was chosen United States Senator, but Greenback members gave their own candidate, Daniel Agnew of Beaver County, sixteen votes.[3]

In the early weeks of the session, the Greenback-Labor members were concerned with two measures vital to labor: "an eight-hour law" and a "store-order bill." A Greenback-Labor Representative, John F. Welsh of Schuylkill County, introduced a bill on February 10, 1879, "limiting a day's work to eight hours." This measure, after committee referral, appeared on May 6, 1879, on the House calendar for third reading; by a vote of 102 to 57 it was indefinitely postponed.[4]

[1] Pennsylvania *House Journal* (1879), 9. Greenbackers Cargill, Conroy, Doyle, Fouse, Morris, Reeder, Seaton, Shear, Thickston, Welsh, and J. B. White voted for Doyle; Gauss, Hines, O'Lenihan, Mooney, and Shoener voted for Henry W. Long, the Republican, elected speaker, while Dewoody voted for D. L. Sherwood, the Democratic candidate.
[2] Pennsylvania *Senate Journal* (1879), 5. J. A. Small, *Legislative Handbook, 1879,* lists Nelson as a Democratic-Greenback and Groff and Paulson as Democrats.
[3] *Ibid.,* 82-83.
[4] Pennsylvania *House Journal* (1879), 174, 204, 211, 235, 249, 817, 960, 961. Ten Greenback members present voted against postponing the bill along with 23 Republicans and 24 Democrats.

In February, Senator T. B. Schnatterly, a Democrat from Fayette County, introduced a "store-order bill."[5] Despite opposition of President *pro tem* Herr of Dauphin County and Senators C. T. Alexander, Democrat of Centre County, and T. C. St. Clair, Republican of Indiana County, it passed the Senate on April 22, 1879, by a vote of 31 to 11.[6] Senators who worked and spoke for the passage of the store-order bill in addition to Schnatterly were George Hall, Democrat, from Elk County, John Parker, Greenback, from Schuylkill County, and J. W. Wilson, Republican, from Venango County. This measure passed the House on May 28, 1879,[7] but was vetoed by Governor Hoyt on June 6. He objected to the bill because he considered it special legislation within the constitutional prohibition and said that "it denied the laborer the right to sell his labor to whom he pleased and for such prices and on such terms that seem good to him without molestation, hindrance, or restriction."[8]

The Greenback supporters were also sympathetic to the several petitions presented to the legislature calling for the reduction of all salaries of public officials.[9] Despite violent protests by Greenbacker legislators and the Greenback-Labor press, the "Tramp Act" was passed, and it received Governor Hoyt's signature on April 30, 1879.[10] This rather severe act provided that any person without a fixed residence, who went from place to place and begged, would be deemed a tramp, would be guilty of a misdemeanor, and would be subject to a prison sentence not to exceed twelve months.[11]

After the legislature adjourned on June 6, the Greenback-Labor Party supporters had five weeks before they convened their State Convention at Altoona, to consider what steps to take to revitalize the movement: whether fusion would be in order or whether independent action should be tried again? The State Greenback-

---

[5] *Laws of Pennsylvania* (1879), 695. This act provided that operatives engaged in and about coal mines, and manufacturers of iron and steel be paid their wages at regular intervals and in lawful money of the United States.

[6] Pennsylvania *Senate Journal* (1879), 695.

[7] Pennsylvania *House Journal* (1879), 1086.

[8] Pittsburgh *Commercial Gazette*, June 8, 1879; Appleton's *Annual Cyclopedia*, 1879, 715.

[9] Pennsylvania *House Journal* (1879), 273, 411.

[10] Much of the violence and damage during the strikes of 1877 was attributed to "tramps."

[11] *Laws of Pennsylvania* (1879), 33.

Labor Party Convention was called to order on July 15 by Frank P. Dewees; one hundred and thirty delegates were present. Dewees, in opening the proceedings, presented an earnest argument against any coalition by the Greenback Party with either of the old parties. Thomas H. Armstrong, of Allegheny County, was elected temporary chairman by acclamation. A committee of fifteen on resolutions and a committee of ten on permanent organization were appointed.[12] Congressman Seth H. Yocum, in answer to calls, made a speech in which he condemned both the Republican and Democratic parties as the common foes of national welfare and contended that if the National party did not step to the front and rescue the country from the sufferings in which the old parties had enthralled it, some other new party would.[13]

Upon reassembling for the afternoon session the Committee on Permanent Organization's report recommending Samuel R. Mason as Permanent Chairman was adopted.[14] Nominations for State Treasurer followed. The names of Henry Carey Baird of Philadelphia, S. S. Weller of Wilkes-Barre, Warren C. Plummer of Crawford, and Peter Sutton of Indiana were presented. All the names except that of Mr. Baird were afterwards withdrawn and he was nominated for the office by acclamation.

The platform presented again called for the replacement of National Bank notes with Greenbacks. The strong pro-labor com-

[12] The Committee on Resolutions was comprised of James E. Emerson, Jacob Krepps, John Tomlinson, Dr. J. C. Taylor, E. M. Davis, Isaac E. Dean, W. W. Heims, E. E. Cotton, W. S. Asldre, John W. Duff, John Bramlie, Thomas Foale, J. C. Schoener, J. S. Coxie, Matthew Murray. The Committee on Permanent Organization was comprised of F. P. Dewees, William Brennen, Peter Herdic, A. L. McFarlane, T. V. Powderly, W. R. Allison, T. W. Taylor, Samuel Calvin, Hiram Moyer, J. Allen Cole. *National Labor Tribune,* July 19, 1879.

[13] Philadelphia *Times,* July 10, 1879.

[14] Other officers included: Vice-Presidents—Charles N. Brumm, Schuylkill; Harry S. Rogers, Berks; J. D. Harris, Luzerne; D. S. Early, Dauphin; James L. Wright, Philadelphia; F. H. Braggins, Mercer; David Kirk, Pittsburgh; S. H. Yocum, Centre; W. B. Barr, Bedford; W. S. Service, Elk; Samuel Calvin, Blair; John A. Brownlie, Butler; Clark Brown, Crawford; I. E. Dean, Venango; H. P. Callow, Washington; J. G. Vale, Cumberland; Joseph D. Dale, Forest; D. W. Lawson, Armstrong; G. T. Warfield, Delaware; John Marsh, Erie; E. S. Watson, Lycoming; John A. Shaffer, Clinton; J. S. Coxey, Montour; T. S. Thompson, Jefferson; William F. Snyder, Juniata; William S. Kountz, Lancaster; Edwin Leeper, Lawrence; J. B. Robinson, Columbia; John Sage, Philadelphia; E. S. Bartell, Philadelphia. Secretaries—Frank M. Smith, F. S. Rock, N. L. McCaw, R. E. Diefenderfer, James McCambridge. *National Labor Tribune,* July 19, 1879.

plexion of the convention became evident in the long list of labor reform planks. The platform demanded a graduated income tax; legislation providing that debts due for labor performed take precedence over all other claims; abolition of the store-order system; legislation compelling the payment, at regular stated rates and in the lawful money of the United States, of all wages due laborers; legislation to prevent all combinations, discrimination or the granting of rebates by transportation companies; a law compelling common carriers to furnish service for the same price to all men. In addition the convention announced that it was opposed to the giving away of the public domain to corporations, and that it favored a free and industrial educational system so that no child would be allowed to grow up in ignorance. Before the platform was adopted several demands were added: that salaries of officials be reduced, that a tariff be imposed on raw materials produced in the United States, that an eight-hour law be passed, and that prison and contract labor be abolished.

After completion of the platform a telegram was received from Henry Carey Baird in which he positively declined to stand as a candidate for State Treasurer.[15] The convention proceeded again to nominate a candidate for the office. The results of the first ballot were S. S. Weller of Wilkes-Barre, 30; Jerome Plummer of Washington County, 38; and Peter Sutton of Indiana County, 48. Mr. Weller's name was then withdrawn. On the second ballot Sutton received 75 votes; Plummer, 13. Mr. Sutton's nomination was then made unanimous.[16]

Frank Dewees retired as State Chairman of the party. He gave as his reason for declining to continue as state chairman the fact that he wished to devote all of his time to the Executive Committee of the National Greenback-Labor Party. The convention named a new chairman. Edward S. Watson, editor of The Wil-

---

[15] Baird gave the following reasons to a reporter for refusing to accept: "Because my business and other pursuits, including my studies on political economy give me all the work that my strength is capable of. I have no political ambition. I did not decline this nomination on account of any falling off in my enthusiasm for the Greenback Party or the Greenback cause." *National Labor Tribune,* July 26, 1879.

[16] Peter Sutton was born in Indiana, Pennsylvania, 1822. He had engaged in various businesses but at this time was living on a farm at Marion, Indiana County. He had been a Democrat until 1846, then a Whig, and a Republican since 1856. After 1876 he was outspoken against the principles of contraction. *National Labor Tribune,* July 26, 1879.

liamsport *National Standard,* was elected on the first ballot with 53 votes; David Kirk of Pittsburgh, polled 32 votes, and T. P. Rynder of Altoona, 9 votes.[17]

This convention did not generate the fervor and enthusiasm of the Philadelphia Convention of 1878. There were reasons: Francis Hughes, since 1876 the outstanding organizer and spokesman for the movement, was absent. His nephew and co-worker, Frank P. Dewees, resigned as State Chairman, and Henry C. Baird of Philadelphia refused the nomination for State Treasurer. All three of these men who now declined to take an active part in the party campaign were respected and powerful leaders in the movement in eastern Pennsylvania; and their actions reflected the loss of interest in the movement there. Eastern agriculture had never been strong in supporting the party, and eastern labor leaders had begun to abandon the state organization. The labor element was at odds with the conservative tendency the party had revealed at the 1878 convention which had rejected the Kilgore labor and currency resolutions; moreover, many of the Philadelphia labor leaders were not friendly to Tom Armstrong, who was now occupying a prominent position in the party's leadership.

Two other factors that affected Greenback strength were increased business prosperity and the lack of enthusiasm in county organizations of the party. General improvement in the nation's economy was reflected in Pennsylvania by increased business in cotton and wool, iron and steel, railroads, oil and leather, and a definite increase in retail sales.[18] By October the completeness of the revival in the national and state economy was reflected in the following editorial in the Philadelphia *Times:*

> The revival of trade has come and it has come to stay until another tide of insane speculation, overtrading, and extravagance shall again halt it. Our labor is employed, our mills, factories, and furnaces are in operation, our crops are abundant, our transportation lines are heavily laden with traffic, our capital is going out with confidence into industrial enterprises, our national credit is firmly established.[19]

[17] Charles N. Brumm, Pottsville, Mayor Powderly, Scranton, and James E. Emerson, Beaver County, were nominated for the office of State Chairman, but declined to run. *National Labor Tribune,* July 19, 1879.
[18] Philadelphia *Times,* September 15, 1879.
[19] *Ibid.,* October 14, 1879.

That business had greatly improved in formerly depressed areas of Pennsylvania can be seen in the following account of improved conditions at Williamsport, Pennsylvania:

> Arrangements have been completed by the firm of Jenkins, Schreyer & Co. to start the Valentine Iron Works at this place, which have been lying idle for a year and a half, and in a day or two they will be in full operation. They expect to employ one hundred men. There is other evidence of the revival of business here. Today Williamsport is in a more prosperous condition than she has been since the panic of 1873. All her manufactories are running, and her box factories and planing mills are so pressed to fill their orders that they are compelled to run nearly all night. Every branch of business is buoyant, and the people feel that good times have come again. Few idle men are seen about the streets. Large lumber shipments are going forward rapidly, and the indications are that the manufacturers will dispose of all their stock this winter. While the price of lumber has not yet advanced, there is a stiffening of the market, which indicates an advance before very long.[20]

Even the *National Labor Tribune* recognized returning prosperity, attributing it, however, to the European crop failures and to the Government's adoption of two Greenback policies, one of coining $2,000,000 monthly in silver[21] and the other of paying $25,000,000 in back soldiers' pensions—measures which had been advocated as National Greenback policy since 1877.[22]

The apathy with which the Greenback-Labor cause was regarded during the summer became evident when fewer than one-half of the counties nominated local candidates.[23] Attempts to raise enthusiasm were made at the opening of the State Greenback-Labor campaign on September 6, when a large rally and a parade nearly three miles long were held at Peter Sutton's hometown of Marion, Indiana County. State Chairman E. S. Watson and James Emerson made speeches in which campaign issues were emphasized.

[20] *Ibid.,* September 21, 1879.
[21] A reference to the Bland-Allison Act of 1878 which required the Government to purchase $2,000,000 to $4,000,000 of silver bullion to be converted into legal tender dollars exchangeable for ten dollars and upward in silver certificates. James F. Rhodes, *History of the United States,* VIII, 94.
[22] *National Labor Tribune,* October 18, 1879.
[23] There is no evidence that any Greenback-Labor candidates met with success in the spring local elections.

The speakers denounced the National Banks[24] and insisted that interest-bearing bonds should be dropped forever; and they called for more Greenback circulation which would reduce interest rates on mortgages from eight percent to three percent. To the acclaim of the crowd they declared for an eight-hour day and demanded a reduction in Government officials' salaries. The "Tramp Act" was denounced and the Governor was berated for vetoing the "Store-Order" bill.[25]

Richard Trevellick, of Detroit, and James Emerson campaigned long and hard in western Pennsylvania. Francis Hughes did not speak but wrote several letters to newspapers for the campaign. One published in Pittsburgh stated, "Whatever measure of relief the workingman has had since 1873 is wholly due to the influence exerted on Congress by the Greenback-Labor Party."[26]

With the Greenback-Labor Party campaigning only in certain areas and with the Democratic Party riddled by dissension, it was easy for the Republican candidate, Samuel Butler, to win the State Treasurer's election with 280,153 votes to the Democrat's Daniel Barr's 222,715 and Peter Sutton's 27,207. The Greenback vote had fallen off two-thirds in a year. In no county did Peter Sutton have a majority, but in Indiana, Tioga, and Warren counties his vote was greater than Daniel Barr's. In only four other counties did Sutton receive a sizable vote: Crawford, Lackawanna, Luzerne,

[24] A popular story in Greenback circles against National Banks was this: "I am a bondholder. In 1864 I had $20,000 in gold. I gave it for $50,000 in Greenbacks and gave them for $50,000 in 5-20 bonds, deposited them with Treasurer at Washington and he gave me $45,000 in blackbacks. I came home and started a National Bank. I loaned the blackbacks to the farmers and of course took a mortgage on their farms. Thus in about four weeks I had $95,000 out on interest. As the law only allowed me 10% interest on loans—deposits in my bank generally amounted to $30,000 on an average, and I generally kept it loaned out; and during all this time my $50,000 in Washington was drawing 6% interest in gold. I always converted the gold into Greenbacks and loaned them, and thus by honesty, economy, and industry, on January 1, 1870, I had mortgage notes of $182,000. Since then I have been swindled by a great many dishonest farmers who mortgaged their land for more than it was worth, and I have been heavily assessed by the Bankers' Union for money for political purposes such as passing laws to strengthen the National credit, so I have been eight years and have only doubled my capital which is now a little over $360,000." Reprinted from *Rural World* in *National Labor Tribune*, September 20, 1879.

[25] *National Labor Tribune*, September 3, 1879. Because wages of the laboring man had been reduced from $10 weekly to $6.00 weekly they could not see, since prices were reduced, why official salaries were not reduced as theirs had been.

[26] *Ibid.*

and Schuylkill. The results revealed that the greatest strength of the Greenback Party now lay in the western section of Pennsylvania and in the anthracite counties, where there was a sizable labor protest vote.

The party, however, did not consider that all was lost, and the *Labor Tribune* berated those who tried to bury it prematurely:

> Our enemies do not look under the surface far enough to observe how much it has restrained the old parties from playing into the hands of the money power, nor how far it has compelled them to adopt its policy. It was the new party that kept down the ultra hard money element, and struck a conservative balance between them. The tubs that have been thrown to the Greenback whale have been the salvation of business. The third party will go on this line until fully successful.[27]

[27] *National Labor Tribune,* November 15, 1879.

CHAPTER VIII

1880. PARTY LEADERSHIP MOVES WEST

The voting strength of the National Greenback-Labor Party in the nation and in Pennsylvania had diminished in 1879, but it remained a potential political threat. Greenback-Labor leaders confidentially expected that they could re-unite the segments of the Greenback and Labor elements into a strong political force for the approaching presidental election. It was accordingly assumed by Thomas Armstrong and other Greenback-Labor leaders that when Pennsylvania State Chairman Watson received an invitation from a Grant Reception Committee to attend a reception for the General in Harrisburg on December 16, 1879, the Greenback-Labor Party was being solicited to support General Grant for the Presidency.[1]

Frank Dewees, Chairman of the National Executive Committee, and T. H. Murch of Maine, Chairman of the Greenback Congressional Committee, agreed in October, 1879, to call a Committee meeting in Washington in January, 1880.[2] The conclave was held on schedule, with twenty-eight states represented and Murch presiding.[3] It decided to hold the National Convention in Chicago, drew up the rules for choosing delegates and issued a "Call to all Supporters of Greenbacks."[4]

In the February election the Greenback-Labor Party won local victories in Scranton, where Mayor Powderly was re-elected, and in Titusville, where William Barnsdale was elected City Treasurer.

---

[1] The Cameron forces were preparing their campaign to secure the Republican nomination of Grant for President at the 1880 convention. *National Labor Tribune*, December 13, 1879.

[2] T. H. Murch to Frank Dewees, October 22, 1879, Dewees MSS.

[3] The *National Labor Tribune* of January 17, 1880, stated "Outside of a few designated as National Committeemen by state committees and the congressmen present, the members represented nobody but themselves." This statement probably was made because Armstrong, the editor, was not invited.

[4] The "Call" signed by Murch and Dewees declared, "Usurious interest and enforced idleness have filled the land with pauperism, misery, and crime, and filled the air with ominous murmurs of discontent. The very foundations of popular government are questioned and assailed and the Republic itself is in danger." *Ibid.*, January 24, 1880.

In the following areas whole Greenback-Labor slates were elected:
Mahanoy, Plane, Coultersville, Cambridge Township in Crawford
County, Connellsville Township in Fayette County, Concord, and
Dunmore Boroughs.[5]

On February 6, Chairman Watson issued a call to the Executive
Committee to meet in Harrisburg to draw plans for the State Convention. The convention opened at Harrisburg on March 23 with
about one hundred delegates. It was described as a "small but
enthusiastic meeting."[6] Francis Hughes served as permanent chairman, and W. C. Plummer, C. N. Brumm, and Congressman Seth
Yocum addressed the Convention.[7] The platform adopted was
brief but contained a change back to a more conservative currency
plank. It stated that "The United States Government shall issue
all currency, gold, silver, and paper, all to be free legal tender
for all purposes, public and private, and there shall be no banks
of issue public or private." This conservative statement was debated for three hours. Opposition to it arose primarily over its
alleged similarity to Democratic statements on currency, but the
majority of the convention agreed with Congressman Yocum when
he maintained that, "the clause is not inconsistent with the
enunciations of the Greenback Party as the Greenbacks are stating
what the Democrats are afraid to say."[8] Other platform planks
declared that nationality, currency reform, and rights of labor were
one and inseparable, and extended sympathy to the workingmen
in California in their efforts to combat the evils of cheap Chinese
labor. The platform for the first time demanded that full restitu-
tion be made to soldiers for the depreciation of money in which
they were paid. It further demanded regulation of interstate commerce by Congress and the maintenance of a tariff for protection
of American industry.[9]

The Convention endorsed Hendrick B. Wright for the Presidential nomination at the Chicago Convention. It also made two

[5] *National Labor Tribune,* February 28 and March 20, 1880.
[6] Philadelphia *Times,* March 24, 1880. This was not the first State Convention in 1880, as the Republicans met in Harrisburg, February 4, and
pledged the state delegation to General Grant's try for the presidential
nomination. *Ibid.,* February 5, 1880.
[7] Brumm in his speech denounced the Democrats in the United States
Senate as "villains" because they did not support Greenback currency. *Ibid.,*
March 24, 1880.
[8] *Ibid.*
[9] *National Labor Tribune,* March 27, 1880.

nominations for state offices:[10] Frank Dewees of Schuylkill County, for Judge of the Supreme Court; and A. S. Roberts of Crawford County, for Auditor General. The following were chosen delegates-at-large to the National Convention: Francis Hughes, Schuylkill; William H. Hines, Luzerne; J. B. White, Warren; and Samuel Calvin, Blair. Alternates chosen were James L. Wright, Philadelphia; F. L. Heath, Erie; D. A. Evans, Tioga; and W. H. Tipton, Adams.[11]

The National Greenback-Labor Convention was called to order on June 9, 1880, by Frank Dewees.[12] This was Dewees' only recorded official act at the Convention, after which he faded from the National Greenback scene. Pennsylvania was credited with fifty-eight delegates among a total of 743.[13] Hendrick B. Wright was placed in nomination by William N. Hines. On the first informal ballot he received 21 votes and on the second, after Butler's withdrawal, he received 129. James B. Weaver of Iowa was nominated on the second ballot. The Pennsylvania delegates split their votes between Wright and Benjamin F. Butler, with only three delegates voting for Weaver.[14] Hughes and Dewees, the apostles of Greenbackism in Pennsylvania, who had been prominent in all previous National Greenback-Labor gatherings, played a minor role in the convention as the forces from the West took over the control and management of the National-Greenback-Labor Party.

The platform adopted at the 1880 convention was comprehensive in its coverage of the grievances of the farmer and laboring man.[15] It demanded that all money, whether metallic or paper, be issued

---

[10] Luzerne delegates to the convention wished to nominate for the Supreme Court, Judge Hardley, a Democrat from Luzerne. It was thought the Democrats would endorse him. It was agreed to withdraw Hardley in favor of Dewees when the convention agreed to endorse Wright from Luzerne for the Presidential nomination. Before Wright was endorsed attempts were made to get Pennsylvania's endorsement for either Samuel R. Mason or Benjamin Butler of Massachusetts. Philadelphia *Times,* March 24, 1880. Tom Armstrong had been promoting Butler for the Presidency since January. *National Labor Tribune,* January 17, 1880.

[11] Philadelphia *Times,* March 24, 1880.

[12] *National Labor Tribune,* June 19, 1880.

[13] Other groups that wished to be represented at the Convention were the Socialist-Labor Party with 44 delegates and the Union-Greenback Party with 187 delegates, Workingwomen with 3 delegates, Kansas workingmen with 3 delegates, and the Eight-Hour League with 6 delegates. *Ibid.*

[14] *Ibid.,* and Frederick E. Haynes, *James B. Weaver,* 160.

[15] See Appendix B for complete platform.

and controlled by the Government and made full legal tender; that labor be protected by National and State authority and that the eight-hour law of Congress be enforced; that more government control of corporations and their practices be made; that a graduated income tax be passed; that the veto power of congressional committees be taken away; that importation of cheap immigrant labor and Chinese serfs be abolished; that the public domain be reserved for actual settlers; that interstate commerce be regulated by the Government; and it denounced the efforts being made to restrict the suffrage.

After Chairman Watson returned from the Chicago Convention to the State Headquarters in Harrisburg, he endeavored to get the campaign in Pennsylvania under way. Funds for the campaign were the first necessity and in a letter to Frank Dewees on July 12 he asked for $800, stating, "Those upon the State ticket have been assessed $800 each. The committee have decided on a stubborn fight, but to carry out their resolutions must be provided with means."[16] In September, Watson organized sectional speaker bureaus, "for surety of speakers and to allow the State Chairman to canvass the State. The following sectional directors were announced: A. B. Finton of Corry to direct speakers for Erie and the northern tier counties; T. P. Rynder, editor of the Altoona *Advance,* to direct speakers in central counties; H. L. Bavers of Harrisburg to direct speakers in central and southern counties; W. L. Hines of Ashley to direct speakers in anthracite counties; and Jacob Duval of Philadelphia to direct speakers in Philadelphia and suburban counties.[17]

Despite enthusiastic reports of response to speakers and of club activity,[18] dissatisfaction was brewing in Pennsylvania Greenback ranks over Weaver's conduct of the National campaign, and it made itself especially evident shortly after the Maine election in September. Pennsylvania Greenbackers were rather jubilant over the Greenback-Democratic fusion victory in Maine on September 11, which resulted in the winning of two of five congressional

---

[16] Watson to Dewees, July 12, 1880, Dewees MSS. No evidence exists of a reply or that Dewees ever mailed any money. Dewees made little effort to campaign.

[17] *National Labor Tribune,* September 11, 1880.

[18] Weaver and Chambers Greenback Clubs were reported in Phoenixville, Elverson, 31st Ward Pittsburgh, Tionesta, Sewickley, Dubois, Reading, Harrisburg, Altoona, Bradford, Fayette City, and Fairchance Furnace.

seats and the election of General Henry Plaisted as Governor.[19]
But controversy developed when the Maine Greenback convention
of September 21 agreed to joint Democratic-Greenback presidential
electors.[20] Solon Chase, leader of the opposition, was a Maine
farmer noted in Greenback annals for his famous statement on
currency and the price of steers. While addressing a Greenback
gathering in Maine he stated, "Inflate the currency and you raise
the price of my steers and at the same time pay the public debt.
Resumption means falling prices and shrinkage of wages."[21]
Chase received 89 votes in 1880 for the presidential nomination
at the Greenback-Labor Convention. He was credited by James
B. Weaver with killing the Greenback Party in Maine by making
it "go straight" and not fusing it with the Democrats.[22] Chase
disagreed so violently with the Convention's action that he created
a "rump" convention which put up a slate of seven Greenback
electors. But Weaver and Murch persuaded him to agree to a
joint electoral ticket made up of four Democratic and three Greenbacks, with Chase as one of the three. When news of this arrangement became known, Francis Hughes sent a protesting telegram
to Weaver. Hughes pointed out that "National Greenback Labor
men are such by principle, and, therefore, not marketable by
leaders," and charged a plot to secure the election of Garfield
electors.[23] Hughes' disgust with Weaver's politics was not improved by Weaver's public reply in which he denied Hughes'

[19] Plaisted had been a Republican until 1877 when he became a Greenback supporter. The Democrats were the Third Party in Maine. In 1879,
the Republicans cast 68,796 votes, Greenbacks, 47,590, and the Democrats
21,688. Reading *Eagle*, September 14, 1880. Weaver's congratulatory telegram to Plaisted derided the Democrats for claiming the Maine victory
as theirs: "It is most amusing to see the Democratic leaders masquerading
behind the Greenback Party and calling our victory a Democratic boom—
a Democrat couldn't come within 40,000 of victory. The Democrats in Maine
showed their good sense by voting the Greenback ticket." *Ibid.*, September
20, 1880.
[20] James Emerson of Beaver Falls spoke to the Maine Greenback Convention of 1,553 delegates. *National Labor Tribune*, June 6, 1880.
[21] Haynes, *Third Party Movements*, 128.
[22] *Ibid.*, 192.
[23] This plan of splitting electors in a Presidential election in several states,
if successful in a close election, would have given the Greenbacks a com-
manding position. It was reported in Indiana that the Democrats and Greenbacks had formed an electoral ticket of 11 Democrats and 4 Greenbacks.
Reading *Eagle*, October 21, 1880.

accusation that he planned to allow the Republican electors to win
Maine:

> We shall see whether Solon Chase or myself have for-
> feited our claims to the confidence of the people by the
> course we have taken in Maine, or whether you have
> forfeited your standing in the Greenback party by slander-
> ing the men who are risking health and even life in
> defense of the right in building up our organization. As
> to your insinuation that I am actuated by sinister motives
> by anything said or done by me during the campaign,
> I denounce you as a slanderer and calumniator.[24]

Before the Hughes-Weaver controversy had time to cool, Dyer
D. Lum's letter of September 29 was made public. Lum, Assistant
Secretary of the Greenback Party, accused Weaver of accepting
$5,000 from the Republican campaign fund.[25] Weaver promptly
denied the accusation and made public his campaign receipts.[26]
These controversies further widened the breach between the Na-
tional Party and Greenback leaders in eastern Pennsylvania. Frank
Dewees as a result on October 5, in a letter to Chairman Watson,
withdrew as the party's candidate for the Supreme Court:

> I have reluctantly come to the conclusion that the original
> purposes of the organization have been subverted by
> General Weaver and other National leaders, who, by
> their national policy are reducing the party to the posi-
> tion of a despised ally of the Republicans, its open and
> vindictive enemy and that in many instances the attempt

---

[24] *National Labor Tribune,* October 2, 1880. Chase had temporarily left
the Maine Democratic Party for the Greenback.
[25] Additional information in F. E. Haynes, *James Baird Weaver,* 167-170,
and Reading *Eagle,* October 2, 3, 1880.
[26] Weaver listed his receipts (*National Labor Tribune,* October 9, 1880).

Chicago *Express*	$ 500.00
American *Sentry*	200.00
Peter Cooper	45.00
Small contributions	500.00
Congressman Murch	50.00
George O. Jones, Albany, N. Y.	800.00
	$2,095.00

Jones was a financial agent of the Greenback Party and according to Lum,
Jones was supposed to have received the $5,000 from the Republican Gov-
ernor of New York. Reading *Eagle,* October 2, 1880.

is now being made to locally use the party as an instrument of barter to subserve personal ambition alone.[27]

Before the November election, Hughes and Dewees were openly supporting Hancock for the Presidency.[28] Both men had originally been Democrats, and Hughes was credited by the New York *Times* with securing the Democratic gubernatorial nomination for Cyrus L. Pershing in 1875.[29] Their action marked the end of prominent eastern influence in the councils of the state party, and it was henceforth dominated by men who represented western agriculture and western labor in Pennsylvania.

Others in Pennsylvania were also leaving the party. Samuel R. Mason in June had announced his return to the Republican Party.[30] During the summer J. R. Blxler dissolved the Greenback organization in Clearfield County.[31] The most telling blow to the National Greenback-Labor Party in eastern Pennsylvania came when James L. Wright, the Philadelphia Anti-Monopoly leader and twice Greenback candidate for state office, announced that "40,000 Greenbackers in Pennsylvania will vote for Hancock. . . . Workingmen can gain more by the Democratic tariff."[32] Schuylkill County proved to be an exception to this prediction, because the Greenback Party again made an agreement with the Republican Party on candidates.[33]

[27] Rumors were prevalent of Weaver's working with the Republicans, by not visiting Republican states, as Ohio, Michigan, and Kansas, but only speaking in the states where he could harm the Democrats. Lum circulated the story that Weaver had a plan of winning the election with Republican aid. If the Democrats were strong in the October elections, in states which held elections in October, such as Ohio and Indiana, the Republicans would then withdraw electors in West Virginia, Missouri, Texas, and Mississippi, in favor of Greenback electors and try to throw the election into the House. *Ibid.,* October 26, 1880.

[28] Hughes whose health was failing devoted his remaining years to his law practice. Dewees abandoned active politics. He considered a new edition of his history of the *Molly Maguires,* but instead moved to Washington, D. C., to practice law and during the Cleveland administration was made an Assistant Attorney General. He also held this office during the Harrison administration. After this, until his death in 1899, he was a successful practitioner before the Court of Claims. Washington *Post,* November 8, 1899.

[29] New York *Times,* October 3, 1876.

[30] Philadelphia *Times,* June 12, 1880.

[31] His reasons: "The Greenback cause has been so bunglingly conducted and the party so multitudinously divided on the simplest questions, faction after faction diverging from the beaten path trod by the regular organization that it is now a sign of want of good sense to see men follow the leadership of a Kearney, Kilgore, or a Dewees." *Ibid.,* June 11, 1880.

[32] Reading *Eagle,* October 20, 1880.

[33] Philadelphia *Times,* October 25, 1880.

In October the split in Greenback-Labor ranks grew wider. On October 19, Chairman Watson and T. P. Rynder of Altoona met in Williamsport with local Greenback supporters and decided to place the name of Samuel Calvin, of Blair County, on the ballot for Supreme Court Judge.[34] But on October 28, a meeting of several state committeemen and a few local leaders took place at Harrisburg without Chairman Watson's presence or knowledge. This group decided to support George A. Jenks, the Democratic nominee for the Supreme Court.[35] When informed of this meeting, Chairman Watson, who was speaking in Shenandoah, declared, "If any committee met at Harrisburg or elsewhere and had attempted to endorse Mr. Jenks or anyone else they did it without official authority. Samuel Calvin was regularly nominated. . . . The Greenback tickets are printed and sent over the state with Calvin's name on it."[36]

The act, however, revealed a split in the executive committee ranks. Watson wanted an independent candidate and did not wish to endorse the Democratic nominee. He was accused, and continued to be accused, during the following year, of favoring the Republican Party. Those members of the committee favorable to the Democrats wished to endorse Jenks. Under the circumstances Calvin did not want his name placed on the ballot, but it was already there and there was little that could be done about it.

The approaching election found the Pennsylvania Republican Party confident, especially in view of the October victories in Ohio and Indiana. The Democrats were not very hopeful but were counting heavily on Hancock's popularity. The Pennsylvania wing of the National Greenback-Labor Party was split, and it was a credit to the Greenback ideal and not to the party organization that it had any success in November.

The election resulted in Republican majorities for all state offices. The Pennsylvania Greenback-Labor vote had shrunk from over eleven percent of the total in 1878 to between one and four-

---

[34] *Ibid.,* October 29, 1880.
[35] To this meeting Samuel A. Calvin sent a telegram, "Under the singular circumstances I will not be a candidate." Reading *Eagle,* October 20, 1880.
[36] *Ibid.,* November 1, 1880. The election date was November 2.

tenths to two and four-tenths percent in 1880. The vote in Pennsylvania was as follows:

	Republican	Democrat	Greenback-Labor
President:	Garfield, 444,704	Hancock, 407,428	Weaver, 20,668
Supreme Court:	Green, 444,934	Jenks, 406,904	Calvin, 12,653
Auditor General:	Lemon, 442,335	Dechert, 405,736	Roberts, 19,226

For Congress the Greenback Party had candidates in all districts except the First and Fourth in Philadelphia, the Sixth in Chester, and the Twentieth in the Centre District.[37] Two Greenback Congressmen were elected: Charles N. Brumm in the Thirteenth, Schuylkill; and James Mosgrove in the Twenty-fifth, Clarion District. Charles N. Brumm was elected from Schuylkill on a Greenback-Republican ticket. During the next twenty-eight years he was re-elected seven more times but did not drop the Greenback label for Republican until after his 1888 defeat. Brumm was characterized as a man who "loved controversy" and his last years spent as a Judge of Schuylkill County were not free from it, since he had to withstand threatened impeachment proceedings brought against him in 1913.[38] In only two other districts did the Greenback candidates make a strong showing; in the Sixteenth district, McKean-Lycoming, David Kirk, now living in Bradford, ran with Democratic support and lost by the small margin of 546 votes; Alf Short, Twenty-seventh, Erie, polled 14,438 votes but lost by 1,302.

In the contests for the State Senate twelve Greenback candidates were in the field, but only one made a good showing: H. K. Sloan, Thirty-seventh, Indiana and Jefferson counties, polled 6,464 votes but lost by 744 votes. For the State House of Representatives, ninety-two Greenback or Greenback fusion candidates tried for the 201 seats, but only two were elected: Francis Miller, Armstrong, on a Democratic fusion, and John F. Welsh, Schuylkill, who won over his Democratic opponent by 24 votes. Green-

---

[37] The Greenback Congressman Seth Yocum did not run. The contest was between Andrew O. Curtin, Democrat, 17,461 votes and Thomas H. Murray, Republican, 14,472. By 1880 the Greenback movement had collapsed in Centre, Clearfield, and Clinton counties.

[38] MSS, Memorial of the meeting of *Bench and Bar of Schuylkill County* for Charles N. Brumm, January 15, 1917, and *Report of the Special Committee appointed to Investigate the Charges Against the Honorable Charles N. Brumm Senate of Pennsylvania*, 1913.

back-Republican fusion was attempted in Lycoming County, where John R. Botts lost by 668 votes; in Northumberland, where John McFarland and John Duttinger lost by 1,605 and 4,058 votes; in Schuylkill's Third district, where John F. Shoener lost by 705 votes. A Greenback-Democrat fusion was tried in Potter, where William Shear lost by 215 votes; in Tioga, where W. T. Humphries and John McKey lost by 1,157 and 4,489 votes; and in Warren, where H. P. Kinnear lost by 735 votes.[39]

Local Greenback-Labor election successes were scored in Schuylkill County where Michael Scanlon was elected Sheriff, J. W. Pomeroy, District Attorney, and G. H. Miller, Auditor; in Mercer County where S. B. Stephenson was elected Surveyor, and in Potter County where Dana Drake was elected Commissioner.[40]

Pennsylvania's 20,668 votes among Weaver's 307,740 placed it fifth in state Greenback voting, behind Missouri, Michigan, Illinois, and Texas, but ahead of Kansas, Wisconsin, West Virginia, and New York.[41]

The Greenback-Labor collapse in eastern Pennsylvania can best be seen by comparing the 1878 vote of twenty-three eastern counties with their 1880 vote. In 1878 they cast approximately 34,000 votes for Mason, but in 1880 they gave only 5,500 votes to Weaver.[42] Four western and northern counties cast over 1,000 votes each for Weaver: Allegheny,[43] Crawford, Indiana, and Tioga. The Greenback Party had its greatest local success in Schuylkill County, where the majority of its candidates were elected.[44]

The 1880 campaign and election clearly indicated that the National Greenback-Labor movement had become largely a western agricultural movement dominated by James B. Weaver, Gilbert De La Matyr of Indiana, and Richard Trevellick of Michigan.

[39] Smull, *Legislative Handbook, 1881*, 270-303.
[40] *Ibid.*, 254-260.
[41] *Tribune Almanac, 1881*, 167. The straight Greenback vote was small in Maine and Indiana, where fusion on presidential electors had occurred.
[42] The 1880 figure includes the 2,488 votes cast in Schuylkill County.
[43] Allegheny cast 1,636 votes, and Philadelphia 237. The above four counties cast 6,034 votes. The *National Labor Tribune*, October 20, 1880, stated, "The small vote is evidence that working men vote for old parties and forsake their principles."
[44] *Ibid.*, November 13, 1880.

They now occupied the spotlight formerly held by Hughes and Dewees of Pennsylvania.

Although the name Greenback-Labor Party was to continue in use nationally, the Pennsylvania movement was to be dominated by labor reformers, with some support from the northern agricultural counties. The currency reformers and political reformers disappeared rapidly after 1880. Several reasons can be cited for this: improved economic conditions, successful resumption, and the split in Greenback-Labor Party leadership which contributed to its failure to gain the kind of successful fusion that was achieved in Maine, Massachusetts, Iowa, and Michigan. In Michigan the Democrats had adopted the main Greenback principles and had absorbed the party.[45] In Maine, after 1877, the Democratic Party became the third party and was willing to cooperate with the Greenback Party. In Massachusetts the Greenback Party under General Benjamin Butler had polled a large vote by joining with the inflation wing of the Democratic Party. In Pennsylvania, despite a large vote in 1877 and 1878, the Greenback-Labor Party clearly remained the third party. The Democratic Party was reluctant to join with the Greenback Party, because it had won the 1877 election without fusion, and many of its leaders believed that an independent Greenback Party would take more votes from the Republicans and thus aid the Democratic cause more effectively. Disgust with the negligible success achieved by 1880 caused more former supporters of the Greenback Party to go back to the older parties, where their vote would not be lost, and to leave the operation of the Pennsylvania party in the hands of certain labor leaders who had scattered support from other reform groups. The party thus continued as a reform party, presenting a nuisance value by threatening fusion with the minority party in certain areas such as Schuylkill County, the western mining regions, and the less prosperous districts of the northern counties.[46]

[45] Haynes, *Third Party Movements*, 192.
[46] After the election, State Chairman Watson tried to instill some new life in the party by publishing a call "To all unflinching Greenback men." The *National Labor Tribune* reported in December that the Greenback congressmen were going to support W. E. "Pig-Iron" Kelley for Speaker of the House because of his favorable tariff views. *Ibid.*, November 20, December 27, 1880.

CHAPTER IX

CHANGING NATURE OF THE PARTY: 1881-1882

For a political movement that did not seem to be going anywhere, there was a surprising amount of Greenback activity in Pennsylvania during the early months of 1881. The currency reformers were still active in 1881, attacking the monetary and fiscal policies of the Government, although resumption of specie payment had been an accomplished fact for two years. Despite improving economic conditions and better farm prices, there was still an active group that wished inflation or greater Greenback circulation, as witnessed by the activity of James E. Emerson, Beaver County manufacturer, who spoke widely in western Pennsylvania on the topic, "The Debt Must Be Paid In Cheap Money."[1]

Agitation continued against the fiscal policies on Government bonds and maintenance of a Treasury surplus; in 1881 Greenback-Labor publications became interested in E. J. Whitehead's petition to Congress which stated that the national debt should be paid with the Treasury surplus and with Greenbacks, and not refunded through the issue of tax free interest-bearing bonds. His petition stated that, "Issues of tax free Government Bonds which deprives us of paying our debt whenever we shall possess the ability, is a direct and unjust system of putting labor under tribute to wealth, and that debt, whether individual or corporate, is an unmitigated curse."[2] This petition, attacking what it termed the unjust share of taxes borne by labor, was circulated on standard petition forms and Greenback supporters were urged by the *Labor*

---

[1] Emerson had figured the National, State, Local, and private debt at $19,280,000,000, which at seven percent annual interest totalled $1,333,360,000 which was greater than the annual earnings of the 11,700,000 workers who averaged $800.00 yearly wages for a sum of $399,400,00, a sum less than interest payments. He stated, "Let your motto be cheap money and well-paid labor will follow. Labor cannot accumulate as interest on aggregate debts outstrip earnings of labor. Your children and children's children will remain poor." *National Labor Tribune,* January 1, 1881.

[2] January 8, 1881. The Greenbackers claimed credit for the Refunding bill passed by Congress in 1881. This bill directed that Government Bonds at three percent interest be accepted by the National Banks instead of six percent Bonds, but President Hayes vetoed the Bill before leaving office. *Ibid.*

Tribune to sign, with the hope that 5,000,000 signatures could be obtained throughout the nation.

Chairman Watson, in December, 1880, sent out a circular letter calling for a re-organization of the party. In order to save the traveling expenses of members, two conferences were held early the next year, one at Oil City on January 19, and the other at Reading on January 26.[3] At the Oil City conference twenty-three counties were represented. The plan of re-organization discussed called for the formation of clubs in every school district that cast votes for Weaver. Clubs were to raise money to pay for speakers to educate the people during the coming campaign. The Reading conference continued the discussion of club organization, and a series of resolutions was adopted which re-affirmed its belief in the Chicago Greenback platform of 1880, recognized the statesmanship and leadership of James B. Weaver as "a fearless exponent of the doctrines of Jefferson and Jackson," and pledged its future support to him. Congressman Brumm was Chairman of the Committee on Resolutions.[4]

Interest was manifested also in the Store-Order Bill, introduced in the Pennsylvania Legislature by Greenback Representative Welsh in the House and another by Democratic Senator Schnatterly in the Senate. Schnatterly's Bill, well-amended, became law on June 29, 1881. This act attempted to secure cash pay days for operatives and laborers in and about coal mines, iron and steel mills and other manufacturers and it provided for the payment of wages at least once a month in cash or in store orders redeemable in cash. In addition, it prohibited excessive profits on goods sold in company stores.[5] This measure, because of its amendments, caused little joy in laboring circles.[6]

In February, 1881, the Greenback Party won a few more vic-

---

[3] Watson's call stated, "Business of the greatest importance will come before these conferences and the State Committee would urge with all earnestness that the several counties send as large a delegation as possible. Other states are moving and why should Pennsylvania remain in the background. Fellow citizens we must re-organize without delay in every city and hamlet, for a well organized enemy confronts us." *Ibid.*

[4] *Ibid.,* February 5, 1881.

[5] *Laws of General Assembly* (1881), No. 173, No. 148.

[6] The *National Labor Tribune* feared the Store-Order Bill could not be enforced. The issue of September 10, 1881, carried reports that workingmen were fired who demanded cash payments. It urged workingmen to strike for enforcement.

tories in local elections in widely scattered towns and townships:
Geneva Borough, Ashland, Girardville, Meadville, Bloomington
Valley, Redstone Township in Fayette County, and Mead Town-
ship in Warren County were among those that reported successful
candidates.[7] April found party leaders engaged in preparing for
James B. Weaver's proposed speaking tour through the oil regions
and to the cities of Harrisburg, Pottsville, Williamsport, and
Philadelphia. The proposed subject of his speeches was "Our
Transition from a Republic to an Aristocracy." He cancelled his
April tour but he did speak in June at Warren and Meadville prior
to the State convention.[8]

On June 15 the State Convention opened at Pottsville with an
address of welcome by Captain William Porter of Minersville and
a reply from Chairman Watson. General Weaver and Gilbert De
La Matyr were featured speakers. The make-up of the Committee
on Permanent Organization of the convention showed the change
in local and state leaders: President, Frank S. Heath, Corry;
Vice-Presidents, James McCambridge, Philadelphia; R. J. Houston, Lancaster; D. W. Stroup, Allegheny; J. L. Dewoody, Venango; V. N. Shaffer, Chester; William Grant, Philadelphia; H. L.
Bowers, Dauphin; L. J. Lilly, McKean; L. W. Gillette, Erie;
Ira Smith, Lycoming; Secretaries, S. P. Brigham, Venango;
Gerald Miller, Philadelphia; W. M. Porter, Schuylkill; A. W.
Smith, Crawford; and J. A. Cake, Northumberland.[9]

The convention nominated by acclamation R. W. Jackson as its
candidate for State Treasurer.[10] It endorsed the National Platform of 1880 and adopted its own statement denouncing the ag-
gregation of real estate by corporations; censured the state legislature for its failure to pass an anti-freight discrimination bill;
demanded protection of American labor and producers; denounced
National Banks for their attempt to coerce Congress by withdrawal
of circulation; indignantly denied the charge of the opposition
press that the Greenback-Labor Party favored an unlimited issue
of currency; declared only such volumes of currency as business

---

[7] *National Labor Tribune*, March 5, 1881.
[8] *Ibid.*, April 2, June 4, 1881.
[9] *Ibid.*, June 25, 1881.
[10] R. W. Jackson lived in West Middlesex Township, Mercer County, and
was a prominent farmer. He ran for the State Senate in 1880 but was defeated. In his letter of acceptance, July 4, he pledged adherence to the Chicago Platform. *Ibid.*, July 23, 1881.

required would be issued; denounced the National Banking system as legalized robbery; and endorsed Weaver and Chambers.

After Watson was re-appointed State Chairman, a resolution was adopted expressing sympathy for the Land League of Ireland and America.[11]

Shortly after the convention adjourned, unsavory rumors concerning Watson began to circulate. It was maintained by some that he was using the office of Chairman of the Greenback-Labor Party to aid the Republicans, and by others that he was mishandling party funds. The executive committee, after meeting in Harrisburg on July 13 to investigate the charges, reported that the charges were unwarranted and announced that it had found nothing to condemn. The committee reported, further, that it placed implicit confidence in his ability and loyalty and resolved that every Greenback paper should publish its findings.[12]

During the summer and early fall Greenback-Labor candidates were nominated for local offices in Allegheny, Blair, Berks, Columbia, Crawford, Fayette, Indiana, Lycoming, Mercer, Northampton, Schuylkill, Venango, Washington, and Westmoreland counties. In Schuylkill County Republican and Greenback conventions met on the same day, September 15, and cooperation continued thereafter when a committee of the Republicans met with a committee of the Greenbackers and decided to divide the county ticket; the Republicans took for their candidates the office of judge, prothonotary, Clerk of Courts, one Commissioner, one Auditor, and Surveyor, while the Greenbacks took the office of Treasurer, Commissioner, Poor Director, Register of Wills, Recorder, and Auditor.[13]

Greenback-Labor campaign troubles developed after Charles S. Wolfe, in September, announced as an independent Republican candidate for State Treasurer. Attempts were made to have Jackson withdraw in favor of Wolfe, and the strength of these efforts can be inferred from the number of denials.[14] Chairman Watson was blamed for attempting a "deal," and the issue continued even

---

[11] Reading *Eagle,* June 16, 1881.
[12] *National Labor Tribune,* July 30, 1881.
[13] The Republican candidates in above order were D. B. Green, G. W. Cole, Morgan Reed, J. R. Davis, R. F. Moyer, G. N. Beadle. The Greenback candidates: Jeremiah Mears, A. J. Shortall, James Grant, John Monahand, Dr. Diffenderfer, and Elias Higgins. Philadelphia *Times,* September 16, 1881.
[14] *Ibid.,* October 8, 12, 1881.

after Jackson denied it in a circular letter on October 12. He stated, "Mr. Watson nor anyone else has the right to circulate any such rumor. I am now and will continue to be a candidate for State Treasurer on the National Greenback-Labor ticket."[15] A meeting of the State Executive Committee followed in Harrisburg, October 14. Chairman Watson, R. J. Houston, A. J. Webster, Frank Heath, and Congressman Brumm were present. Brumm presented this resolution: "That the malicious rumor of withdrawing Jackson is unfounded and originated in Philadelphia. We pledge full support to him, and State Chairman Watson shall communicate this to Jackson."[16] Watson was again endorsed by the committee.[17]

Before the election Greenback leaders estimated that the party vote would be in excess of the 20,000 cast in 1880,[18] but the Greenback candidates received only 14,946 votes or two and six-tenths percent of the total. The regular Republican candidate, Silas M. Bailey, won with 265,293 votes, while Charles S. Wolfe, the Independent, polled 49,969. The Democratic candidate, Orange Noble, received 258,387 votes. In no county did Jackson make a strong showing. The vote in counties where he had most success was: Schuylkill, 1,641; Crawford, 1,245; Indiana, 1,204; Allegheny, 1,015; Venango, 933; Lycoming, 571; Philadelphia, 254; and Northumberland, 131. In Schuylkill County, the Democrats won all the offices except Judge,[19] thus halting the success of the Greenback-Republican fusion.

The Greenback-Labor Party retained its name during 1882, although there was an attempt to change it at the State Convention.[20] The party, which now embraced anti-monopoly[21] and labor

---

[15] *National Labor Tribune,* October 15, 1881.

[16] *Ibid.,* October 22, 1881.

[17] Watson's future action would indicate his desire to cooperate with the Republicans, for in 1882 he wrote from Binghamton, New York, where he was employed as a type setter, to General James A. Beaver, the Republican candidate for governor, and offered to work in General Beaver's behalf. He offered to publish two pamphlets—one attacking the Greenback leaders, the other praising General Beaver. Candidate Beaver was to pay the cost of publication. No record of payment nor of the pamphlets is in evidence. Edward S. Watson to James A. Beaver, June 5, 1882. James A. Beaver MSS.

[18] Philadelphia *Times,* October 20, 1881.

[19] *Ibid.,* November 10, 17, 1881.

[20] A motion was tabled to change the name to The National Party. The Reading *Eagle* in its accounts of the State Convention calls it a convention of the National Labor Party. Reading *Eagle,* May 19, 1882.

[21] The Anti-Monopoly League was active during 1881. A mass meeting was held in February at Cooper Union protesting the pooling of railroad

reform principles as well as the Greenback, began to make its campaign plans early in 1882.[22] James Weaver was encouraged to speak in Pennsylvania and began plans for a tour in late February.[23] Members were also following the progress of currency bills in Congress, where Brumm, on January 23, 1882, introduced a measure to facilitate the payment of the public debt and to establish a uniform currency.[24] This bill was buried in the House Banking Committee, and a bill extending National Bank charters for twenty years was reported.

The State Executive Committee met in Harrisburg on March 29, 1882. Secretary A. J. Webster called the meeting to order and T. P. Rynder, Altoona, presided. It was reported to have been the largest turnout of the committee since 1877. Since E. S. Watson had been removed as chairman by the Executive Committee "for cause," particularly for his friendly attitude toward the Republicans,[25] Frank Heath of Corry was chosen to act as State Chairman until the May State Convention.[26] A committee of eleven headed by Tom Armstrong, of Pittsburgh, was appointed to raise money for the campaign. The Executive Committee decided to nominate a full state ticket, although some members wanted the party to concentrate on congressional candidates.[27] Before the State Convention took place, Chairman Heath, on May 3, gave an address before the National Executive Committee at St. Louis. He spoke on Greenback prospects in Pennsylvania now that the two old parties were in chaos. It was at this meeting that a "call"

and telegraph lines. *National Labor Tribune,* February 26, 1881. Studies on the operation of the Standard Oil Company began in the March issue of the *Atlantic Monthly.*

[22] Several meetings of the Allegheny County Greenback Committee were held in February and March. Three Greenback men had been elected in February to the Common Council on the citizen's ticket. *National Labor Tribune,* March 4, 25, 1882. In Reading, several members reported, "that if it had not been for President Gowen's letter keeping in force the order preventing employees of the Reading Railroad from occupying political positions more ward tickets would have been nominated in Reading." Reading *Eagle,* February 20, 1882.

[23] He required a fee of $25.00 plus local and hotel expenses. He cancelled his engagements in February until after April. *National Labor Tribune,* February 25, 1882.

[24] *Ibid.,* January 28, 1882.

[25] Reading *Eagle,* May 17, 1882.

[26] Heath was editor of the Corry *Herald* and in August, 1881, received a license to preach in the Methodist Church. Philadelphia *Times,* August 15, 1881.

[27] *National Labor Tribune,* April 4, 1882.

to all party supporters was prepared, with 2,000,000 copies to be printed. An invitation was extended to the Land Leagues, Farmers' Alliance, Anti-Monopoly League, and the Knights of Labor to join the National Greenback-Labor Party.[28]

The State Convention met in Harrisburg on May 18, and the platform adopted reflected an attempt to appeal to all of the previously mentioned groups.[29] A short currency plank was placed in the middle of the platform. It declared opposition to the monopoly of the National Banking system, to the monopoly of telegraph and transportation, and to the monopoly on land. It demanded a revision of the tariff to protect American labor, justice in the administration of pensions for the Civil War soldiers, government issue of all currency, and the eight-hour day.[30]

Before this platform was adopted, Frank Heath was made permanent State Chairman and the following candidates were nominated: Governor, Thomas A. Armstrong, Allegheny; Lieutenant Governor, Terence V. Powderly, Luzerne; Secretary of Internal Affairs, Thomas Dewoody, Venango; Supreme Court Judge, J. Adam Cake, Northumberland; Congressman-at-Large, Robert K. Tomlinson, Berks.

Before adjournment it was resolved that the Executive Committees should consist of the County Chairman and one member from each Senatorial District and that the State Committee could remove any candidate by a two-thirds vote.[31]

During the summer several independent labor conventions were held. Among them were a county convention in Pittsburgh on July 11, and a State Labor convention in Philadelphia on August 28. The latter was attended by 125 delegates, including Frank Heath. A. C. Rankin served as chairman of the Committee on

[28] *Ibid.*, June 3, 1882.
[29] E. M. Davis, one of the original Greenbacks from Philadelphia, published a letter in the Philadelphia *Public Ledger*, March 1, 1882, in which he decried that most of the original Greenbackers had left the party and many "isms" were now attached. He concluded with "Many of us are busy using our money teaching our doctrines rather than upholding party machinery." Reprinted *ibid.*, April 5, 1882. Henry Carey Baird in a letter to the Philadelphia *Inquirer*, September 20, 1882, predicted, "the Greenback ideas are the ideas of the future for a people so intelligent, so practical, and so enterprising as Americans."
[30] *National Labor Tribune*, May 27, 1882.
[31] *Ibid.*, and Reading *Eagle*, May 19, 1882.

Resolutions.[32] Fifteen resolutions were adopted, fourteen on labor reform and one on currency. After considerable debate a resolution was adopted 82 to 23 to support Armstrong for Governor.[33]

In the counties where organizational strength remained there was increased activity over 1881. Tom Armstrong Clubs were formed in the Pittsburgh area, and county conventions put forth slates of candidates in Allegheny, Armstrong, Beaver, Clarion, Crawford, Dauphin, Fayette, Forest, Green, Indiana, Jefferson, Lawrence, Lycoming, Mercer, Schuylkill,[34] Tioga, Venango, and Washington counties.[35]

During the campaign the question arose as to where the Greenback-Labor Party was getting the money to have so many speakers in the field when generally the party was financially hard-pressed.[36] The Democrats charged that the Greenbackers were getting their money from the Republicans. Democratic Chairman Hensel accused Heath of accepting Republican money to finance Greenback campaign speakers in Democratic counties. The *National Labor Tribune* on November 4 denied both this charge and the accusation that Armstrong had sold out to the Republicans. How much truth there was to the accusations cannot be truly ascertained, but Armstrong was formerly a Republican and the party did not seem to be having financial troubles after July.

[32] The committee on permanent organization: Isaac Cline, Chairman; Vice-Presidents; John Jarrett, President, Amalgamated Association of Iron and Steelworkers; Miles McPadden, Organizer, Knights of Labor; Hattie Curran, L. A. No. 1468, Philadelphia; Simon Waldman, Tailors Union, Philadelphia; Major Stirling, Garfield Pioneer Assembly No. 1684; James White, D. A. No. 40, Clearfield; Secretaries: C. L. Dodd, Brotherhood of Carpenters, Philadelphia; and F. A. Borell, D. A. No. 3, Venango; *ibid.,* September 2, 1882.

[33] Reading *Eagle,* August 28, 29, 1882.

[34] The Greenback organization had been almost entirely taken over by the Republicans. Brumm ran for Congress on a Greenback-Labor-Republican ticket. In the twenty-fifth Congressional District, Congressman Mosgrove refused the Greenback nomination.

[35] Reading *Eagle,* July 15, 22, August 19, 20, September 2, 9, 16, 1882; Philadelphia *Times,* July 21, October 2, 1882.

[36] Allegheny County committee was assessed $25.00 in April by Heath and it was reported "money was badly needed." It was proposed also that everyone who voted for Weaver in 1880 send $1.00 to Heath to raise a campaign fund of $20,000. *National Labor Tribune,* April 15, 1882. At the April meeting the Allegheny County committee discussed hiring an organizer to get members. They needed $75.00 weekly for the organizer. It was proposed that seventy-five members give $1.00 weekly for this purpose, but the idea was dropped when only twenty members were willing to contribute. *Ibid.,* May 6, 1882.

Republican State Chairman Thomas Cooper wrote to James A. Beaver in August and mentioned the excessive amount of money the Republicans would have to raise to wage a successful campaign. He mentioned also that the Republicans had had a hand in the nomination of Thomas Armstrong as the Greenback candidate for governor and "that the Independent Republicans because of this are liable to run fourth behind the Democrats and Greenbacks."[37] If the Republican leadership expected the Greenback-Labor Party to poll more votes than the Independent Republicans, one may conjecture that the Republicans had more than a passing interest in the conduct of the Greenback-Labor campaign.

The election results were disappointing to the Republicans; if, as seems likely, the Republicans contributed to the Greenback campaign, their disappointment was no doubt bitter. The election results were as follows: Governor: Robert E. Pattison, Democrat, 355,791; James A. Beaver, Republican, 315,589; John Stewart, Independent Republican, 43,743; T. A. Armstrong, Greenback-Labor, 23,996.

In ten counties in which Armstrong had the greatest support he polled the following vote: Allegheny, 4,587; Schuylkill, 2,061; Indiana, 1,286; Tioga, 939; Venango, 908; Westmoreland, 807; Erie, 772; Warren, 676; Philadelphia, 672; and Crawford, 605.

For Congress seventeen Greenback-Labor candidates tried for seats in Congress, but all lost except Brumm, who defeated his Democratic opponent by 624 votes. For the State Senate all eight Greenback-Labor candidates were defeated. Only forty-nine attempted to win seats in the House and all were defeated. Except for two in Schuylkill, these candidates ran in the northern and western counties. The Greenback Party was without representation in the 1883 session of the Legislature.[38]

Armstrong was disappointed at his small vote, and he spoke plaintively about the laboring man who voted for the old parties and not for principles. His bitterness was understandable, since the Greenback-Labor Party had run a "straight labor ticket."[39] He consoled himself, however, by pointing out that the Prohibition Party had received but ninety-nine votes in Philadelphia, where there were over three hundred ministers of the Gospel.

[37] Thomas Cooper to James A. Beaver, August 31, 1882, Beaver MSS.
[38] Smull, *Legislative Handbook, 1883*, 687-707.
[39] *National Labor Tribune,* November 11, 1882.

If there had been any doubts about the matter, the 1882 election demonstrated clearly that the Greenback-Labor Party was not going to be a strong third party in Pennsylvania. The campaigns showed the increased tension, which had been growing since 1878, between those who favored fusion and those who would have nothing to do with the old parties. The more conservative and practical, by 1881, had gone back to their old parties and left in charge agricultural and labor reformers largely centered in northern and western Pennsylvania. It has been asserted that a majority of Greenback-Labor votes returned to the Democratic Party, and that this fact helped to account for its nationwide successes in 1882;[40] but in Pennsylvania the Independent Republican movement was the determining factor.

[40] Haynes, *Third Party Movements*, 144.

CHAPTER X

THE PARTY'S LAST YEARS: 1883-1887

Reform was in the air during the national elections of 1882. The espousal of reforms, most of them political, had enabled the Democrats to carry the House of Representatives and they elected governors in thirteen of the sixteen state contests. Republican factional battles over spoils helped bring about this result, but the failure of the Republicans to guard governmental integrity was an additional factor. In this period of better conditions for the populace, the currency reformers were still active, for in January, 1883, the National Currency League issued a call for "a conference of citizens who favor immediate currency reform" to meet in Washington on February 7:

> Citizens [regardless of past political affiliations] who earnestly desire to see all the circulating mediums of the country issued and controlled by the National Government, without intervention of National Banks or other private corporations should attend.

Those who planned to attend were to notify either Congressmen T. H. Murch, I. S. Hazeltine, C. S. Brumm or one of the other Greenback members in Congress, and, in addition, the Central Division of the National Currency League in New York City.[1] The meeting, which was attended by all Greenback members of Congress, was called to order on February 7 by Wallace P. Groom. Permanent Chairman was Edward M. Davis, of Philadelphia; Thomas P. Rynder of Altoona served as one of the secretaries.[2]

In Pennsylvania during the early months of 1883 there were some doubts as to the future value of continuing the currency and labor reform issues in a political movement, because dwindling voters, internal party strife over party policies, and attempted bargains by leaders with other parties made the Greenback Party's prospects unpromising for that year. Without too much optimism,

[1] *National Labor Tribune,* January 13, 1883.
[2] *Ibid.,* February 24, 1883.

State Chairman Heath, after consultation with the State Central Committee,[3] called a meeting for May 2, at Harrisburg, at which the future of the party in Pennsylvania would be considered, the resignation of the chairman would be tendered, and an effort would be made to aid in pushing the labor bills then before the State Legislature. Heath, endeavoring to take credit for labor reform away from the Democratic Party, in the following party call, gave the Greenback-Labor Party full credit for the labor legislation being considered during the 1883 session of the Legislature:

> Workers of this party were the only political agitators of any party in the state that dared before the last election to advocate the rights of labor and to condemn the encroachment of monopolies. Since convening of the Legislature little other than labor and anti-monopoly legislation has been passed or discussed. It would be a public calamity should this fearless anti-monopoly organization cease its agitation and work. In view of these circumstances therefore the chairman takes liberty to invite leading men throughout the State, without regard to party, who are resolved to act against the evils of anti monopoly in all its forms . . . to meet at the same time and place to consider future action for the welfare of the state.[4]

This appeal to anti-monopolists and other groups brought only nineteen men to the meeting. Letters were read from Henry C. Baird of Philadelphia and Edward M. Davis of Montgomery County urging the party "to stand firm to its principles," and a resolution was passed censuring William Howard of Bethlehem as "unworthy of confidence of the National Party," because he had published a letter on the eve of the previous November election in which he charged Tom Armstrong with fraud, because Armstrong had printed tickets of the other parties with his name at the head of their tickets for Governor.[5] Heath presented his financial report, which showed expenditures for the 1882 campaign of $1,946.49 with income of $1,644.24, leaving a deficit of $302.74 owed him. He then resigned, and T. P. Rynder of Altoona was

[3] *Ibid.,* April 14, 1883.
[4] *Ibid.,* April 21, 1883.
[5] Philadelphia *Times,* May 3, 1883.

chosen state chairman.[6] In spite of the small attendance, the meeting decided to hold a state convention at Williamsport in August.

Little local Greenback activity was evidenced in the months that followed,[7] but in June considerable comment was heard in Greenback-Labor Party circles concerning the large number of labor reform and anti-monopoly measures passed by the State Legislature. The bills passed provided for education of children in almshouses, abolished the contract system of labor in prisons and regulated the wages of inmates, discharged prisoners in jail under the insolvent act, provided for security and health of miners in bituminous coal, prevented consolidation of competing pipe lines, required anthracite coal operators to keep ambulances for conveyance of injured miners, required owner, lessee, or foreman of every anthracite coal mine to furnish props and timber for the safe mining of coal.[8]

The bills indicated the beginning of advocacy of labor reform by the Pennsylvania Democratic Party.[9] These measures were particularly heartening to the leaders of the Greenback-Labor Party in Pennsylvania, for since 1879, they had been more interested in the grievances of labor than in experimentation with currency.

The two outstanding reform measures passed were the Wallace Arbitration Act and the Anti-Discrimination Act.[10] Labor reform

---

[6] *National Labor Tribune,* May 12, 1883. Rynder was a trade-unionist who was editor in Altoona of a Greenback-Labor paper, *The Advance.* His home was in Milesburg, Pa., and he was a persistent candidate for office until 1890 when he was the labor candidate for Governor polling 224 votes.

[7] Allegheny County Executive Committee reported a poor turnout at its June 30 meeting. *Ibid.,* July 7, 1883.

[8] *Laws of Pennsylvania* (1883), 111, 112, 99, 101, 61, 155, 125, 45, 53, 108, 109.

[9] The House was Democratic and the Senate Republican.

[10] The Wallace Act provided that the Judge of Common Pleas or the President Judge in chambers, upon the petition of 50 workmen employed by five different firms, or five employers who employ at least ten workmen each, or a firm employing 75 men, shall appoint a tribunal of an equal number of employers and workmen, for the adjustment of disputes in the iron, steel, glass, textile, and coal trades. If after three meetings the tribunal was unable to make a decision, an umpire should be selected, "by the mutual choice of both employers and workmen constituting the tribunal," who shall decide the points submitted to him in writing within ten days. The decision when made may be made a matter of the Court's record when submitted to the proper judge, who endorses his approval and directs it to be entered on record. When so entered it shall be final, and the proper court may, on motion of any interested party, enter judgment thereon. The Anti-Discrimination bill stated, undue and unreasonable discrimination to be unlawful and that, "no railroad company or other common carrier engaged in the transportation of property shall charge, demand, or receive from any person

measures considered but defeated were an eight-hour law, a bill to incorporate trade unions, a personal liability law, and a law to compel payment of wages every two weeks.[11]

On August 9, T. P. Rynder issued a call for the Greenback State Convention. He appealed to all groups, including merchants and businessmen, with the hope of once more attracting many from these groups who had supported the party in 1877-1878. His appeal stated, "Let the farmers, laborers and merchants assemble and assert their rights against the encroachment of confederated monopolies of money, transportation, land and labor. Write to me for excursion tickets."[12] About forty attended the convention at Williamsport.[13] Rynder called the meeting to order and Reverend William K. Crosby of Warren gave the opening prayer. Permanent officers were: Chairman, Thomas D. Armstrong; Vice-President, Justus Watkins, Crawford; Secretaries, G. A. Miller, Philadelphia, and H. W. Stein, Lancaster. The convention was addressed by Armstrong, Brumm, and J. A. Sanborn, of Horseheads, New York. The platform committee, consisting of S. L. Youngman of Philadelphia, R. J. Houston of Lancaster, C. F. Walsh of Schuylkill, Justus Watkins and D. W. Whitney of Warren, presented a platform that condemned the issuance of paper money by national banks and recommended that all paper money be issued by the Federal Government. The convention made the following nominations: State Treasurer, H. T. Marsh of Erie; Auditor General, T. P. Rynder, Blair.[14]

Little campaigning was done, and local activity developed only in Allegheny, Beaver, Crawford, Dauphin, Indiana, Schuylkill, and Warren counties. It was generally accepted that the party had slight chance of winning statewide offices, but the rank and file took consolation in the party's accomplishments, which were reviewed from time to time in the remaining Greenback press. Lee Crandall, now national secretary of the Greenback-Labor Party, issued a review that was typical:

> Greenback agitation long ago put a stop to the contraction of currency by preventing cancellation of greenbacks.

or corporation . . . a greater sum than it shall charge or receive from any other person or corporation. . . ." *Laws of Pennsylvania* (1883), 15, 72.
[11] *National Labor Tribune*, April 28, May 26, 1883.
[12] *Ibid.*, August 18, 1883.
[13] Connellsville *Keystone Courier*, September 7, 1883.
[14] *National Labor Tribune*, September 8, 1883.

The party has compelled the Secretary of the Treasury
to issue certificates both of gold and silver which are a
shabby travesty of greenbacks. It has concentrated opposition to the encroachment of incorporated wealth,
and though so far the money power has out-voted us at
the polls, the supporters of greenback ideas, the ideas
themselves alone give all the potency there remains in
either of the old war-parties.[15]

The remnants of the party took heart from articles of this kind
and received encouragement from Rynder's "call to action" issued
from Altoona, on October 25:

Your chairman appeals to you to stand by your post at
this election, now more than ever since '77-78 are your
principles discussed. Opposed to this monopolistic hard
times policy is the greenback policy. . . . You are standing
on the eve of the worst panic your country ever saw,
unless it be modified or averted by the adoption of your
principles. . . .[16]

Appeals of this kind might have been more effective if they
had reached more people, but the daily newspapers no longer carried news of the Greenback-Labor Party, and the leaders were
dependent for publicity on the remaining Greenback and Labor
weekly newspapers, such as the *National Labor Tribune,* Altoona
Advance, Ebensburg *National,* Greensburg *Issue,* and Indiana
Banner.

For the first time since the party's organization in 1876, its
candidates polled fewer votes than the Prohibition Party's nom-
inees. Marsh received 4,431 votes and Rynder 4,452, while the
Prohibition candidates received over 6,000 votes. The Republican
candidates won the offices of Auditor General and State Treasurer.

As we have seen in Pennsylvania and it was true in the nation
as well—agitation for currency reform had diminished to the point
of insignificance. The reformers among farmers in the West and
workingmen in the East, by 1884, were shifting the emphasis of
their attack to the development of big business and monopolies.
This fact is demonstrated by the preface to the Greenback platform of 1884: "Never in our history have the banks, the land

---

[15] *Ibid.,* October 13, 1883.
[16] *Ibid.,* November 3, 1883. Business failures had increased during 1883.

grant railroads, and other monopolies been more insolvent in their demands for further privileges—still more class legislation. In this emergency the dominant parties are arrayed against the people and are abject tools of corporate monopolies."[17]

The Presidential campaign in 1884 brought a moderate revival of interest in the Pennsylvania Greenback-Labor Party. Encouraged in March by the decision of the United States Supreme Court affirming the constitutionality of Greenback money, county leaders began making plans to select delegates for the National convention. Rynder worked to secure a full state delegation to the convention. He did not succeed. He planned to hold a state convention with the delegates at Pittsburgh on May 26, but his purpose was thwarted because excursion tickets to the National convention prohibited stopovers.[18]

Fifty-seven delegates[19] were selected by the State Executive Committee or by county conventions to attend the Indianapolis convention. T. A. Armstrong and T. P. Rynder, delegates-at-large, served as leaders of the delegation. The National Convention of the Greenback-Labor Party opened at Indianapolis on May 28 with 611 delegates present. James B. Weaver served as permanent chairman. After James Weaver and Thomas Armstrong withdrew their names, Benjamin Butler, of Massachusetts, was nominated for President.[20] The platform was prefaced with a review of the party's accomplishments:

> We point with pride to our eight-year history: We forced the remonetization of the silver dollar; prevented the refunding of the public debt into long time bonds; secured the payment of the bonds, until the "best banking system the World ever saw" for robbing the producers, now totters because of its contracting foundation. We have stopped the squandering of the public domain upon corporations; we have stopped the wholesale destruction of greenback currency; and secured a decision of the Supreme Court of the United States establishing forever the right of people to issue their own money.

[17] Philadelphia *Times,* May 29, 1884.
[18] *National Labor Tribune,* May 3, 1884.
[19] *Ibid.,* May 24, 1884.
[20] Butler had been nominated on May 10 by the anti-monopoly convention. No Vice-Presidential candidate was selected. The choice was left to the Executive Committee who in August chose General Absalom M. West of Mississippi. Philadelphia *Times,* August 17, 1884.

The platform demanded the substitution of Greenbacks for National Bank notes, the destruction of "land, railroad, money and other gigantic corporate monopolies," the restoration to the public domain of lands granted to railroads, prohibition of alien ownership of land, regulation of interstate commerce, a government postal telegraph, a graduated income tax, abolition of the convict labor systems, the fostering of public education, reduction of the hours of labor, the abolition of child-labor, prohibition of the importation of contract labor, and reduction of the term of Senators.[21]

Butler played a wary game before accepting the Greenback nomination.[22] On June 12, he issued a letter covering five columns of fine newspaper print in which he discussed practically every question but the one relative to his acceptance of the Greenback nomination.[23] After Butler had attended the Democratic convention as a delegate and had received little attention there, he accepted by letter from Massachusetts, on August 12, the nomination of the Greenback convention.[24] His letter expressed the hope that the dissatisfied elements could be consolidated into a People's Party.[25] Butler made two campaign speeches in Pennsylvania: one at the Granger's Picnic at Williams Grove, Cumberland County, late in August, the other at Pittsburgh on October 10. Butler Clubs were active in western Pennsylvania, notably in Allegheny, Westmoreland, Crawford, and Indiana counties.

The State convention of the National Greenback-Labor Party (now occasionally referred to as The People's Party) was held

[21] *National Labor Tribune,* June 7, 1884.
[22] His reply of May 28, to J. W. Begogle, Indianapolis, who wired him if he would accept the nomination. "Thanks for your consideration but why should I be asked a question which under the circumstances was never put to any other man? Is not my record as a Greenbacker for twenty years sufficient without a formal pledge to you which would cause me to be pointed to as a man who bids for the nomination?" Philadelphia *Times,* May 29, 1884.
[23] *National Labor Tribune,* June 21, 1884. Armstrong who was a strong supporter of Butler called this letter, "a square acceptance of the Indianapolis nomination," but nowhere does Butler seriously hint at accepting the nomination.
[24] Haynes, *Third Party Movements,* 149.
[25] E. H. Gillette, chairman of the National Greenback-Labor Party reported in July that it was absolutely false that General Butler would support the Democratic nominee, "His appearance at the Chicago convention was to urge the Democratic Party to adopt those great principles, the advocacy of which made him our candidate." He opened to that party, "the door to immediate success by uniting with working people of the United States rather than with Wall Street." *National Labor Tribune,* July 26, 1884.

in the Bush House in Bellefonte on September 30. M. K. Foster
of Bellefonte gave the opening prayer and Thomas St. Clair of
Indiana served as chairman. Speeches were made by Brumm,
Armstrong, St. Clair, T. W. "Old Beeswax" Taylor of Homestead and Andrew W. Curtin, who visited the meeting. Rynder
was continued as State Chairman for another year with two vice-
chairmen—James W. Breen in Pittsburgh and N. F. Campion
in Philadelphia. A resolution was adopted supporting General
Butler, presidential electors were chosen, and N. T. Atwood of
Venango was nominated for Congressman-at-large. A platform
was adopted which contained some new issues among its planks:
that the tax for voting be abolished, that Federal officeholders
be elected by the voters of the district, and that employer's liability
laws be passed. A novel departure from conventional procedure
for the party in Pennsylvania was the appointment of a committee[26] to meet with a similar committee of one of the other
parties to form a joint electoral ticket. This motion was bitterly
debated before it was passed and was amended to require that
fifteen of the electors should be of the Greenback or People's
Party.[27]

Greater political interest was demonstrated than had been shown
in the previous year, with more meetings being held, mostly in
western Pennsylvania, and as a result Butler polled 17,002 votes
in Pennsylvania; this was over 1,200 more votes than the Prohibition candidate, St. John, polled. Atwood, the Congressional
candidate, polled 9,684. The vote of the ten leading counties for
Butler was as follows:

Allegheny	2,687
Schuylkill	1,426
Crawford	1,190
Indiana	1,186
Philadelphia	778
Venango	687
Tioga	680
Westmoreland	557
Mercer	518
McKean	501
	10,210

[26] The make-up of the committee: Rynder, St. Clair, Armstrong, Frank
Quick, Wesley Chambers, J. S. May, and James Breen.
[27] *National Labor Tribune,* October 4, 1884.

For Congress, Charles Brumm, Schuylkill, on a Greenback-Republican ticket, defeated his Democratic opponent by over 1,200 votes. For the State House of Representatives candidates ran in only eight districts. Robert Dudley, of Westmoreland County, running on a Greenback-Republican ticket, was elected to the House. Greenback-Labor candidates for the State Senate were presented in only Armstrong, Blair, Butler, Cambria, Chester, Lawrence, Mercer, and Venango counties, and all ran third.[28]

During the first months of 1885, two congratulatory rallying appeals were published in the Greenback-Labor press: one from State Chairman Rynder, the other from the National committee. Rynder's January appeal stressed the economic situation and optimistically forecast a rising future for the party:

> I beg leave to congratulate you on the fact that your party organization has been carried through the dangers of the past two years. Your party name and principles have been maintained. Your vote of 4,452 in 1883 was increased to 17,002 in 1884. You are now in a position to make a grand forward movement for the relief of labor and business. . . .

> The past year showed the unprecedented record of 11,600 business failures with $224,000,000 of liabilities. . . . This year opens with 447 failures in the first week and 420 in the second—a record unprecedented in financial history.

> Your party is the only one that has a practical plan of relief and you have never needed it as now. . . . Dangerous movements to break down the labor organization are on foot. Dangerous efforts are being pushed to demonetize silver and thereby contract the currency.

> Only a distinct notice of our party power will overthrow these movements against the prosperity of business and labor. Let us give the notice at the Spring election.[29]

The appeal of the National committee was based on the premise that the National Greenback-Labor Party was the only political party that made any attempt to grapple with the evils "flooding the country," and that all of the economic evils could be traced

---

[28] Smull, *Legislative Handbook, 1885,* 475-604.
[29] *National Labor Tribune,* January 24, 1885.

to Congress' "infamous financial legislation of the past quarter of a century."[30]

But the Greenback-Labor upsurge called for by Rynder in the Spring election did not materialize. To keep the movement alive he issued a notice for a state convention at Erie for August 12. His summons began with a rousing claim: "Never has a minority party accomplished as much as ours, and never have labor and business had such need of our industrial and financial principles as now. . . ."[31] The State convention was called to order by Rynder in the Erie Courthouse. H. L. Bunker of Blair served as permanent chairman; S. G. Barnes of Indiana and G. O. Perry of Erie served as secretaries; A. T. Marsh of Erie and George Van Fleet of Jefferson as county assistants.[32] M. A. Leary of Schuylkill and N. L. Atwood of Venango spoke to the gathering. Congressman Brumm was not present, but William Wilhelm of Schuylkill reported Brumm was at home tending the legal needs of some laboring men. They adopted a platform that "reaffirmed the Indianapolis platform of 1884." No new provisions were among the adopted resolutions. After Wesley Chambers and S. G. Barnes withdrew their names, W. D. Whitney was nominated for State Treasurer.[33] There was little campaign activity following the convention.[34] The biggest rally was held on October 19 in Pittsburgh when Jesse Harper of Illinois spoke and urged the voters "to join hands with those of the Greenback-Labor Party to better the conditions of the people."[35]

That the party's fortunes had reached a low ebb was attested to by a notice on October 24 in the *National Labor Tribune*: "Friends of Party in Allegheny County desiring to contribute

[30] *Ibid.,* March 21, 1885. The appeal was signed by E. H. Gillette, Chairman, and B. W. Terlinde, Secretary.
[31] *Ibid.,* June 27, 1885.
[32] The Committee on Credentials: S. P. Bingham of Venango, Dr. W. D. Whitney of Erie, Jefferson Sweeney of Mercer, Daniel Duffy of Schuylkill, A. M. Orr of McKean, W. C. Coburn of Forest, and T. P. Rynder of Centre. The Committee on Permanent Organization: T. A. Armstrong, H. M. Close of Beaver, George Van Fleet, Michael Nogle of Bedford, A. T. Marsh, John K. Ray of Blair, and A. J. Shortull of Schuylkill.
[33] *National Labor Tribune,* August 22, 1885.
[34] Fusion had ended in Schuylkill County. "The Greenback-Republicans who have been running on the fusion plan in Schuylkill County have decided to separate. The Republicans have seceded from the plan laid down by a joint committee and refuse to be bound by their action." *Ibid.,* October 24, 1885.
[35] *Ibid.*

toward printing tickets for our party this fall, will please forward money to J. H. Stevenson, chairman, at once." Rynder, in the same issue, informed prospective voters that the state tickets were ready and friends could secure a supply by addressing T. P. Rynder, Milesburg, Pennsylvania. Allegheny County members could secure them at the *Labor Tribune* office. To vote the ticket it had now become necessary to write for a ballot or get it at the *Labor Tribune* office in Pittsburgh.

The party made its poorest showing in the 1885 election. W. D. Whitney polled only 3,569 votes. M. S. Quay, Republican, was elected State Treasurer, while the Prohibition Party's candidate, Barr Spangler, polled 15,074.[36]

The party's political influence was now at a very low point, and during early 1886 party action was confined almost entirely to the efforts of T. P. Rynder. He wrote a letter to President Cleveland in April urging him to alleviate the conditions of the workingmen by issuing more currency, regulating the railroads, and recovering all possible public lands. A reply from Cleveland's secretary telling Rynder that his letter had been referred to the Secretary of the Treasury was the only direct result, but Rynder had this letter published wherever he could find a newspaper that would print it.[37]

In June the State Executive Committee issued a call for a state convention in Harrisburg on August 18. Since the Democratic convention was also scheduled for the same place at the same time, some Republicans contended the Greenbackers were trying to make a trade. This was denied and the *National Labor Tribune* stated, "The party will stand or fall on its principles."[38] But on August 5, Rynder and the Executive Committee, evidently satisfied that no advantageous arrangement could be consummated, announced the postponement of the Greenback convention until September 16. After the Democratic convention met in August, an editorial in the *National Labor Tribune* commented on the excellency of the Democratic candidates: "Take it all in all the Democrats have swung around laborwise to an extent heretofore unknown with the old parties. The candidates, Maxwell Stevenson, W. J. Brennan and Chauncey F. Black, are all friendly to labor."

[36] Philadelphia *Times*, November 14, 1885.
[37] *National Labor Tribune*, May 22, 1886.
[38] *Ibid.*, June 19, 1886.

At the Harrisburg State convention, Congressman Brumm served as permanent chairman. The committee on credentials reported 139 delegates from thirty-six counties. The question of supporting candidates of other parties was widely debated but the convention arrived at no conclusion on this matter. The Schuylkill County delegates, where fusion had worked very well, evaded the issue by stating, "We never endorsed any of the old parties, the old parties endorsed us." The Convention's platform invited all citizens who desired equal rights to support it and the party, denounced the contraction policy of the Treasury, demanded forfeiture of unearned railroad land, absolute protection of American labor, a graduated income tax, the repeal of the labor conspiracy laws in Pennsylvania, advocated a "practical" eight-hour day and co-operatives, urged that labor of children under fifteen be prohibited, and demanded weekly payment of workers.[39] The Convention nominated the following candidates: for Governor, Robert J. Houston of Lancaster;[40] for Lieutenant Governor, John Parker of Schuylkill; for Auditor General, Daniel S. Early of Harrisburg; for Secretary of Internal Affairs, Seth Hoagland of Mercer; for Congressman-at-Large, Clark D. Thompson of Oil City.[41]

There was some campaign activity by local candidates in Allegheny, Blair, Crawford, Indiana, and Northumberland counties, and the vote on a statewide basis improved slightly over 1885. However, the Republican candidates for state offices all had substantial majorities. Houston polled 4,835 votes.[42] His vote was

[39] The platform committee: J. D. Pyatt of Lancaster, T. A. Armstrong of Allegheny, Daniel S. Early of Harrisburg, Joshua A. Burroughs of Susquehanna, James Silvees of Columbia, J. S. Kirchner and William Shetzline of Philadelphia. *Ibid.*, September 25, 1886.

[40] Houston was born in Londonderry, Ireland, in 1832 and came to Lancaster County as a boy. He successfully organized several businesses: Conestoga Cork Works, Helvetia Leather Company, and a Notion business in 1870 that was successful for thirty years. A former Republican in politics he joined the Greenback Party in 1877. In 1886 he was President of Branch No. 694 of the Irish League of America at Lancaster and was a member and later President of The Irish Federation of America. "Mr. Houston, although assisting liberally all deserving religious, charitable, and educational institutions had not united with any Church." John H. Beers, *Biographical Annals, Lancaster Co.*, 240-242.

[41] John Parker was a blacksmith by trade and edited the *Mahanoy Record*. Daniel Early, a Greenback worker since 1876, was an insurance agent. Seth Hoagland was a farmer. Clark Thompson was a physician and a nephew of John Brown. *National Labor Tribune*, September 25, October 16, 1886.

[42] Charles Brumm was re-elected to Congress as a Greenback-Republican candidate.

greatest in Indiana, Northumberland, and Schuylkill counties. The Prohibition Party's candidate for Governor, Charles S. Wolfe, polled 32,458 votes, a clear indication that the Prohibition Party had replaced the Greenback-Labor Party as the third party in Pennsylvania.[43] Although the party's influence had practically disappeared, after the election some attempts were made to find solace and gain credit for the party's accomplishments. As the *National Labor Tribune* declared, The Greenback-Labor Party was not successful in securing office, but it was successful as a minority party in "its influence upon legislation and administrators."[44]

In 1887 the remaining members of the party turned their attention to the Union Labor Movement.[45] In January the National Chairman of the Greenback-Labor Party called for an Executive Committee meeting at Cincinnati on February 21, 1887, simultaneously with the convention of the Union Labor Party. His call pointed out that "an independent political organization is being formed to unite all forces of producers. We must do all in our power to help this movement."[46] On January 29 Rynder echoed the sentiment with a notice calling attention to the Cincinnati Convention and urging that the Greenback-Labor Party of Pennsylvania be well represented.[47] In Pennsylvania the jointure was completed at the first State convention of the Union Labor Party at Williamsport on September 7, 1887. The meeting was called to order by T. P. Rynder. A committee of thirteen, with Charles Brumm as chairman, was appointed to write a platform. T. P. Rynder was chosen chairman of the state committee and George S. Boyle of Shenandoah its secretary. At this convention Charles S.

[43] The Prohibition Party had placed a Greenback plank in its platform in 1885.
[44] *National Labor Tribune,* November 13, 1886.
[45] *Ibid.,* November 20, 1886. T. A. Armstrong was a member of the thirteen-man executive committee that called this convention. B. S. Heath, Chairman, called on members in the states to appoint state chairmen and organize at once. *Ibid.,* November 27, 1886.
[46] *Ibid.,* January 22, 1887.
[47] *Ibid.,* February 5, 1887. E. D. Benedict of Bradford County had been appointed state organizer for Pennsylvania. Each congressional district was allowed one delegate from each of the following organizations to the Union Labor Convention: Soldiers Organizations, Agricultural Wheels, Farmer's and Laborer's co-operative unions, People's Party, Anti-Monopoly Leagues, Grange, Farmer's Alliance, Greenback-Labor Party, Trader's Unions, and Knights of Labor. Also all other organizations in sympathy. *Ibid.,* January 15, 1887.

Keyser of Philadelphia was nominated for the Supreme Court and H. L. Bunker of Hollidaysburg for State Treasurer.[48]

Thus the Greenback-Labor Party lost its identity in the Pennsylvania political scene by joining with a new third party. This jointure did not engender a revival of political interest in Pennsylvania, since the largest Union Labor vote was 8,902, cast in 1887. The following decade spawned several new political parties, most important of which was the People's Party, which received only 8,714 votes in Pennsylvania in 1892. In 1896, the year of many candidates and parties, the combined vote in Pennsylvania for the candidates of the Prohibition, People's, Socialist-Labor, National, and Jeffersonian Parties was 38,930, considerably less than the 82,000 protest votes cast for the Greenback-Labor candidates in 1878. Not until 1912, in Pennsylvania, did a third party enjoy the popularity of the Greenback-Labor Party.

[48] *National Labor Tribune*, September 17, 1887.

CONCLUSION

The Greenback theory of a widely circulating paper currency, not based on specie, had its antecedents in the early history of the United States. Prior to the Civil War people had become accustomed to state and private bank notes circulating freely for all domestic transactions. Government-issued paper money had been used in colonial America as early as 1690, when Massachusetts issued its first Bills of Credit. Coin in circulation in America was never sufficient to meet the demands of business, and various kinds of paper money were used in all stages of the nation's development. Faith in the government, state, or private issuing agencies determined whether or not the paper money circulated at par or below par. Often colonial governments, and later state banks, issued an excessive amount of paper money without any plan of redemption for the amount issued. The plan of the Greenbackers called for an expansion of currency according to credit needs and a contraction of Greenbacks when the Federal Government found them in oversupply by converting them to government bonds.

The currency situation became acute after 1865 because of the disappearance of the state bank notes after the imposition of the ten percent tax on them. National bank notes did not solve the currency difficulty because they were scarcest when needed most and were plentiful in lush times when their abundance led to speculation.[1] Since national bank notes did not meet the credit needs of the western farmer, he turned to Greenbacks as a means of securing relief from his financial burden of low prices and high interest rates. Since the Federal Government did not pay in specie between 1862 and 1879 and for all practical currency purposes was off the gold standard, except for paying bond interest in gold, it was not unnatural for the indebted farmer to call for a controlled currency such as government-issued Greenbacks. This currency was to be based on land value, as were the earlier colonial bills of credit. When paper currency had been issued in larger volumes in the past, relative prosperity had been enjoyed by busi-

[1] Shanon, *The Farmer's Last Frontier,* 315.

nessmen and farmers. Ready loans at low interest rates as proposed by the Greenback theorists were particularly acceptable to labor. It was expected by labor leaders that a low interest rate on government bonds would dissuade capital from investing in government bonds and induce it to invest in industry; this action, it was thought, would bring greater business activity and higher employment. Loans at low interest also would enable labor to secure the necessary funds to set up producer co-operatives. Why then, reasoned the farmer and laborer, would not a government-issued paper currency based on interconvertible government bonds at low interest rates bring prosperity?

Eastern bankers and conservative business leaders, with the exception of high-tariff Greenbackers like Peter Cooper and Henry Carey, opposed the Greenback theory. Many of these men were making a profit on the world gold exchanges in the transfer of gold bullion following trade balances. They were also the holders of large amounts of Government securities bearing an average of five to seven percent gold interest. Thus they were fearful that a large new issue of Greenbacks would have an unsettling effect upon world trade in gold and upon foreign investments in this country. Actually, these fears were not completely justified, since foreign investments had been heavy in the years prior to 1860 when state bank notes flourished and fluctuated, and gold had kept its independent value during the Civil War, when Greenbacks were first issued.

The world depression that started in 1873 was first severely felt on the United States money markets in September, 1873. It touched off a long series of business failures with the ensuing drying up of credit, which was reflected in falling prices and widespread unemployment.

Greenback advocates, disappointed with the Republican and Democratic handling of the monetary problem organized an Independent, or National, Greenback Political Party. This party planned to solve the financial problem by having the government issue more Greenbacks, which would become the national currency, along with silver coins. National Banks and their notes would be abolished and financial control of monetary affairs would be taken out of the hands of the private bankers and their functions replaced by the Federal Government. By these measures the Greenbackers hoped to stabilize the nation's economy and improve the financial situation for the farmer and laborer.

In Pennsylvania until 1876 Greenback idealists and supporters looked primarily to the Democratic Party as the political group that would bring about currency reform, but with the cancellation of the Greenback plank in the 1876 State platform, several prominent Democrats, Francis Hughes, Victor Piollet, and Frank Dewees, began to drift from the party and to flirt with the budding Greenback political movement. The party in Pennsylvania had gained considerable political power by election time in 1877. The party had combined prominent Greenback supporters from the old parties with agricultural and labor leaders, so that its vote of 52,000 in an off election year was the largest state Greenback vote in the nation and put Pennsylvania to the forefront of the movement for the crucial nationwide congressional and gubernatorial elections of 1878.

Three factors prompted Pennsylvania's strong Greenback movement: prominent leadership, severe agricultural depression in sections of Pennsylvania, and the extreme distress of laborers, particularly the miners of Pennsylvania.

The leaders of the party in Pennsylvania in 1877-78 were a heterogeneous group, representing almost every station of life: prominent Republican and Democratic politicians, laborers and union leaders, farmers, and Grange officials, and Greenback philosophers.

Severe depression in prices for farm produce, lumber, and tanbark brought strong support for the movement from the northern counties, while the strongest labor support for the movement came from the laboring men most affected by strikes and unemployment —the coal and iron ore miners of Pennsylvania.

The Greenback Party in Pennsylvania has been accused of various deceptions in its period of existence. Several bear mentioning: that it was formed by the Democrats to take away votes from the Republicans; that it was controlled by the Republicans, who picked its candidates and financially supported the party to "hamstring" the Democrats. The precise truth in the matter is, of course, difficult to ascertain. A politician's thinking from year to year frequently defies analysis, and his reasons for doing things are just as hard to fathom. Moreover, when political agreements or "deals" are made, recording of their having occurred is often studiously avoided. However, the available evidence does point out the following concerning the question of fusion of the Greenback Party: the party did not, as happened in Iowa, Maine, and Massachusetts, join in a statewide fusion. In 1877-78 the leadership of the party may have inclined toward the Democratic Party, but the make-up of the Greenback Party was so diffused and varied that it is doubtful whether the party could have been kept united if the leaders, Hughes and Dewees, had attempted an open statewide fusion. An additional factor militating against fusion was the lack of unity in Democratic Party strategy, largely because of the differences between the Wallace and Randall factions of the party. The Wallace forces were against fusion, while Randall seemed to favor it. Another point that must not be over looked is the fervent optimism with which some of the Pennsylvania Greenback leaders anticipated the growth of the Greenback-Labor Party into a national organization, as the Republican Party had grown in 1856, and the disappearance of one of the older parties by 1880. With such a vision of greatness for the Greenback-Labor Party, these men naturally opposed fusion with the older parties. However, the very make-up of the party soon shattered this dream.

Deals by the Greenback-Labor organization in local areas were quite often made with startling results for the party which had previously been in the majority. The leaders of the major parties were often more interested in preventing fusion that would be damaging to them than in effecting fusion that might have benefited them.

After 1879 there is evidence that suggests Republican control of the party. Watson, the Greenback state chairman, leaned toward the Republicans and he was removed from his state chairmanship for this reason. In 1882, Chairman Cooper of the Republican Party claimed to have had a part in the selection of Thomas Armstrong, labor leader from Pittsburgh, as the Greenback-Labor candidate for governor, much to the consternation of the Democrats and Independent Republicans. The Greenback-Labor Party's vote after 1882 became so small that neither major party was much concerned with its activity.

Pennsylvania occupied a prominent place in the National Greenback-Labor movement from 1877 to 1879. It held the spotlight in the national movement jointly with Iowa. Francis Hughes, of Pottsville, was prominent in setting up the national strategy and directed his nephew and protege, Frank Dewees, who served as chairman of the National Executive Committee from 1878 to June 1880. Hughes and Dewees were conservative Greenbackers. The fact that they showed more concern for the problems of labor than for those of agriculture was not calculated to please westerners, but Pennsylvania's large vote and Hughes' prominence kept them in the forefront. Hughes served as permanent chairman of the Toledo convention of February, 1878, and he undoubtedly had a part in the indefinite, watered-down currency statement of the Union platform, but the pro-labor statements of the platform appealed strongly to the laboring man. It was at this convention that Greenbackers and Labor joined under the name of the National Greenback-Labor Party. Western resentment of their influence was noticeable at the party's National Convention in 1880, when James B. Weaver assumed control of the party as the champion of the western farmers. Hughes and Dewees openly broke with Weaver during the campaign and returned to the Democratic Party before the 1880 election.

The threat of the Greenback-Labor Party to the older parties declined rapidly after 1879. Commonly cited as the reasons for this decline are the return of prosperity and the successful resumption of specie payments on January 1, 1879. Prices did rise on agricultural products, but only briefly, because they were to tumble to new lows in the 1880's. Labor and management had not settled their differences, and low wages, strikes, and labor strife were to continue. Thus what "prosperity" agriculture and labor enjoyed was at best, temporary or intermittent, and it cannot be regarded as an important reason for the languishing of Greenback-Labor support. There were more immediate causes for the party's decline. Break-up of the National party's organization should be noted. Although the party was to continue in name as the Greenback-Labor Party until 1887, each state's organization became a separate entity. Attempts to stir up nationwide enthusiasm after 1879 brought little response from the voter. Lack of unity among state and national leaders was in evidence everywhere. It was even difficult to hold a state organization together; leaders were constantly changing and new faces were taking over leadership. In Iowa, the home state of James B. Weaver, there were two Greenback parties by 1885—one for Weaver, one against him.

The fact that labor practically deserted a labor political party figured in the party's rapid decline in influence. Labor was concentrating intensely on solving its problems through strengthening its labor organizations, either by a strong national union as attempted by the Knights of Labor, or by more numerous and stronger national craft unions. The vast majority of the leaders in these two labor movements lost interest in and took little part in the activities of the Greenback-Labor Party after 1878. They were too engrossed in developing their own philosophies of unionism, through which they sought to rectify many of the workingman's problems. Labor, for all practical purposes, had renounced interest in an independent labor political party.

Another factor that took support away from the Greenback-Labor movement was the espousing of labor reform by the Democratic Party after 1880. The first start toward constructive labor reforms in Pennsylvania were made during the Democratic administration of Governor Pattison, 1883-1887.

The 1882 election in Pennsylvania showed the workingman's indifference to a labor political movement. Tom Armstrong, the outstanding labor leader remaining in the Pennsylvania Greenback-Labor movement, was the party's candidate for governor. His total vote was less than ten percent of the total union membership of Pennsylvania.

Even if the workingman was interested in casting a ballot for a labor candidate, he had to overcome three obstacles before voting: first, he had to have a tax receipt, for either property or poll tax; second, he had to have the proper party ballot (each party printed its own and in its last years the Pennsylvania Greenback-Labor Party had difficulty securing money to print its ballots); third, voting was open and the voter was therefore exposed to the pressure of his employer or a ward leader who, presumably, would not look with favor upon the labor candidate.

After 1878 the majority of the original supporters of the Greenback-Labor movement in Pennsylvania were voting with the Democratic and Republican parties. Eastern and anthracite labor leaders took a smaller part in Greenback-Labor activities and transferred their interest to the Knights of Labor or to promoting craft unions. Except for scattered votes in the anthracite region, as, for instance, in Pottsville, where the Republicans and Green-backers fused, the majority of the party's votes by 1879 came from western Pennsylvania counties and those counties on the Northern Tier along the New York state border. The farmers in these counties were to continue to give a relatively strong vote to the party until its demise. The other votes of the party came from the bituminous coal fields, where company stores existed and cash pay days were infrequent. Some additional votes came from union members, such as the Amalgamated Association of Iron and Steel Workers in Western Pennsylvania, because of the influence of Tom Armstrong, editor of the association's trade paper, *The National Labor Tribune*.

Although the career of the Greenback-Labor Party was brief and its immediate impact upon national politics was not great, the movement had a genuine significance which did not cease with the disappearance of the party. At the height of its strength, it acted as an irritant, a goad, to the major parties. Thus, by agitation, by the dissemination of thought, by disturbing the equanimity of both Republicans and Democrats, it served the good purpose which many claim for all third parties: alerting the major parties to the voice of the people, and forcing a greater measure of integrity and responsibility from the government. Many Greenback ideas and policies were adopted by both Republicans and Democrats, either in their original or in modified form.

The regulation of interstate commerce, free public education, the income tax, the control of business combines, the abolition of prison contract labor, and the use of subsidies for ship building and for public works were advocated in Greenback-Labor platforms. Long after the party had died out, these Greenback measures for which the Greenback-Labor Party had striven were signed into law.

In their advocacy of a credit expansion policy, the Greenbackers were fifty years ahead of their time. It was not until after the passage of the Federal Reserve Act in 1913 that there was any attempt to control credit expansion and contraction on a nation-wide scale. World War I brought about further credit expansion. Still further credit expansion was made possible by the nationalization order of 1933, because under it gold was no longer money but "the psychological reserve"[2] behind federal reserve note currency, the basic medium of circulation after 1933. It is interesting to speculate upon the possible consequences if the Greenback-Labor Party had succeeded in securing credit expansion. This might have turned the clock of history ahead, brought about an earlier industrial and commercial growth, hastening the international complications which set off World Wars I and II. On the other hand, such acceleration of the growth of our wealth and power might have given the United States an international stature great enough to forestall these wars.

As this study has attempted to show, much of the nature of the Greenback-Labor movement and a good share of the impetus which it received nationally must be attributed to the political activities of Pennsylvania Greenbackers. More than is usually recognized, Pennsylvania provided the ideal soil for nourishing the seeds of the movement. Its great labor force and large agricultural area responded with a vigor unknown in most other states to the exigencies created by expansion and recurrent economic distress. Moreover, Pennsylvania provided leaders with stature and political acumen who for a time were able to mold Greenback supporters into a formidable state party and who had a strong voice in national councils of the party. Whatever the verdict of history concerning the place of the Greenback-Labor Party in American political and economic development, Pennsylvania must bear a good share of the responsibility for the character of this phenomenon of American politics.

[2] Shultz and Caine, *Financial Development of the United States*, 675.

BIBLIOGRAPHY

BIBLIOGRAPHICAL AIDS

A Checklist of Pennsylvania Newspapers, Harrisburg: Pennsylvania Historical and Museum Commission, 1944.

Bining, Arthur C., *Writings on Pennsylvania History,* Harrisburg: Pennsylvania Historical and Museum Commission, 1946.

Biographical Directory of the American Congress, Washington: Government Printing Office, 1950.

Commons, John R. *et al.,* ed., *A Documentary History of American Industrial Society,* 10 vols., Cleveland: Arthur H. Clark Co., 1910.

Larrabee, Lillian A., *Description of the James Addams Beaver Manuscript Collection,* State College: Pennsylvania State University Library, n.d. (Typewritten copy).

Levin, Bernard S., ed., *Pennsylvania Historical Records Survey,* Philadelphia: Historical Society of Pennsylvania, 1940.

Stevens, Sylvester K., *Pennsylvania Sources in Various Western Depositories,* Harrisburg: Pennsylvania Historical and Museum Commission, 1949.

MANUSCRIPT MATERIALS

James Beaver MSS (in Pennsylvania State University Library).

MSS of Memorial Meeting of the Bench and Bar of Schuylkill County for Charles N. Brumm (in Historical Society of Schuylkill County).

Frank Dewees MSS (in Historical Society of Schuylkill County).

The Loeser Family MSS (in Historical Society of Schuylkill County).

Samuel J. Randall MSS (in University of Pennsylvania Library).

OFFICIAL DOCUMENTS

Compendium of the Tenth Census, 1880, 2 vols., Washington: Government Printing Office, 1883.

"Industrial Statistics, 1880-81," *Annual Report of the Secretary of Internal Affairs of the Commonwealth of Pennsylvania,* Part III, Legislative Document No. 8, Harrisburg: Lane S. Hart, 1882.

Journal of the House of Representatives of the Commonwealth of Pennsylvania, 1879, 1881, 1883, 1885, Harrisburg: Lane S. Hart, 1879-1885.

Journal of the Senate of the Commonwealth of Pennsylvania, 1879, 1881, 1883, Harrisburg: Lane S. Hart, 1879-1883.

Laws of the General Assembly of the State of Pennsylvania, 1879, 1881, 1883, 1885, Harrisburg: Lane S. Hart, 1879-1883.

Report of the Transactions of the Pennsylvania State Agricultural Society, 12 vols., Harrisburg: State Printer, 1854-1877.

State Board of Agriculture, Agriculture of Pennsylvania, 17 vols., Harrisburg: State Board of Agriculture, 1879-1894.
Tenth Census of the United States, 1880, 22 vols., Washington: Government Printing Office, 1883, III.

NEWSPAPERS

Coudersport *Potter Journal,* 1877-1880.
Connellsville *Keystone Courier,* 1882-1884.
Greensburg *Pennsylvania Argus,* 1876-1882.
Harrisburg *Telegraph,* 1875-1880.
Harrisburg *Daily Patriot,* 1877-1880.
Lancaster *New Era,* December, 1878.
Mercer *Sandy Lake News,* 1878-1881.
New York *Times,* 1876-1877, 1880, 1881, 1882.
Oil City *Derrick,* 1877-1881.
Philadelphia *Press,* October, 1878.
Philadelphia *Public Ledger,* September 1, 1876-December 30, 1878.
Philadelphia *Times,* 1875-1887.
Pittsburgh *Commercial Gazette,* 1877-1879.
Pittsburgh *Daily Post,* 1876-1879.
Pittsburgh *Evening Chronicle,* July 1-December 31, 1878.
Pittsburgh *National Labor Tribune,* 1876-1887.
Pottsville *Miners Journal,* 1878-1879.
Reading *Daily Eagle,* 1877-1884.
Scranton *Daily Times,* 1876-1878.
Somerset *Herald,* 1876-1881.
Titusville *Herald,* 1878-1880.
Warren *Mail,* 1875-1879.
Washington (D. C.) *Post,* 1898.
Washington (Pennsylvania) *Reporter,* 1878-1880.
Wellsboro *Agitator,* 1877-1880.
Williamsport *Sun and Lycoming Democrat,* 1876-1879.

PAMPHLETS

Barns, Charles R., *Proceedings of the Missouri State Greenback Convention,* 1877, St. Louis, 1877.
Berkey, William, *The Monetary Question, The Legal Tender Monetary System of the United States,* Grand Rapids, 1876.
Bolles, Albert S., *What Kind of Currency Shall We Have?* (n.p.), 1883.
Carey, Henry C., *Contraction or Expansion,* Philadelphia, 1866.
———, *Currency Inflation: How It Has Been Produced and How It May Profitably Be Reduced. Letters to the Hon. B. H. Bristow, Secretary of the Treasury,* Philadelphia, 1874.
———, *The Public Debt,* Philadelphia, 1866.
Cooper, Peter, *A Letter on the Currency: To the Editors and Legislators of My Native City and County,* New York, 1875.

Davis, Edward M., *To the Friends of a Greenback Currency* (n.p.), 1880.
Gardwell, Godek, *Currency: The Evil and the Remedy,* New York, 1846.
———, *Usury: The Evil and the Remedy,* 1843.
Greenback Q.E.D., New York, 1879.
Hill, Britton A., *Absolute Money: A New System of National Finance, Under a Cooperative Government,* St. Louis, 1875.
Jones, John P., *Coinage of Silver Dollars,* Washington, 1878.
Kelley, William D., *Money and National Finance: An Address Delivered by Request of Citizens of Philadelphia, January 15, 1876,* Philadelphia, 1876.
Kulp, George B., *Hon. Hendrick Bradley Wright,* Wilkes-Barre: Wyoming Historical and Geological Society, 1881.
Lowery, Morrow B., Hon., *Speech on the National Bank Question, The Bonds of Our Government, The Currency and Tariff, and the Revenues of the Government,* Harrisburg, 1868.
Nourse, B. F., and Jerons, W. Stanley, *Silver Question, Papers Read Before the American Social Science Association,* Saratoga, September 5, 1877.
Schilling, Robert, "History of the People's Party," *Official Souvenir of the National Convention of the People's Party at St. Louis, Mo.,* Milwaukee, 1896.
Searching Analysis of the Action of Paper Money on the Trade and Prosperity of the United States, San Francisco, 1868.
Van Buren, John D., *How to Resume Specie Payments Without Contractions: A Letter to the Secretary of the Treasury,* New York, 1865.
Wanamaker, John, *Speeches of John Wanamaker on Quayism and Boss Domination of Pennsylania Politics* (n.p., n.d.).

MISCELLANEOUS COLLECTIONS

Appletons' *Annual Cyclopedia and Register of Important Events of the Year,* 43 vols., New York: D. Appleton Company, 1872-1903, New Series Vols. III, IV, V, VI, VII, VIII, IX, X, XI, 1879-1887.
Smull, John A. and William P., *Legislative Handbook, 1874-1888,* Harrisburg: Lane S. Hart, 1875-1889.
Tribune Almanac and Political Register, 67 vols., New York: Tribune Association, 1856-1914.

GENERAL HISTORIES

Oberholtzer, Ellis P., *A History of the United States Since the Civil War,* 5 vols., New York: Macmillan Co., 1917-1937.
Rhodes, James Ford, *History of the United States from the Compromise of 1850,* 8 vols., New York: Macmillan Co., 1892-1932.

STATE AND LOCAL HISTORIES

Bausman, Joseph H., *History of Beaver County, Pennsylvania,* 2 vols., New York: Knickerbocker Press, 1904.

Beers, John H., comp., *History of Schuylkill County,* 2 vols., Chicago: J. H. Beers & Co., 1916.

Blackburn, E. Howard, *History of Bedford and Somerset Counties,* 3 vols., New York: Lewis Historical Publishing Co., 1906.

Bradsby, Henry C., *History of Bradford County, Pennsylvania,* Chicago: S. B. Nelson & Co., 1891.

Craft, David, *History of Bradford County, Pennsylvania,* Philadelphia: L. H. Everts & Co., 1878.

Davis, Torring S., *A History of Blair County, Pennsylvania,* Harrisburg: National Historical Association, 1931.

Dunaway, Wayland F., *A History of Pennsylvania,* New York: Prentice-Hall, 1935.

Hand-Book of Petroleum, 1859-1898, 4 vols., Oil City, Pa.: Derrick Publishing Co., 1898.

History of Cumberland and Adams Counties, Pennsylvania, Chicago: Warner Beers, 1886.

Linn, John B., *History of Centre and Clinton Counties, Pennsylvania,* Philadelphia: L. H. Everts, 1883.

Meginness, John F., *History of Lycoming County, Pennsylvania,* Chicago: R. C. Brown & Co., 1892.

————, *History of Tioga County,* Chicago: R. C. Brown & Co., 1897.

Munsell, E. H., *History of Schuylkill County,* New York: W. H. Munsell, 1881.

Oberholtzer, Ellis P., *Philadelphia: A History of the City and Its People,* 4 vols., Philadelphia: S. J. Clarke, 1912.

Pennypacker, Samuel W., *Pennsylvania in American History,* Philadelphia: W. J. Campbell, 1910.

Schenk, J. S., ed., *History of Warren County,* New York: D. Mason & Co., 1887.

Sipe, Chester H., *History of Butler County, Pennsylvania,* Indianapolis: Historical Publishing Co., 1927.

Biographies

Beers, John H., *Armstrong County, Pennsylvania: Her People, Past and Present,* 2 vols., Chicago: J. H. Beers & Co., 1914.

————, *Biographical Annals (Lancaster County),* Chicago: J. H. Beers & Co., 1903.

————, *Commemorative Biographical Record of Central Pennsylvania,* Chicago: J. H. Beers & Co., 1898.

Carman, Henry J. et al., ed., *The Path I Trod,* New York: Columbia University Press, 1940.

Collins, Emerson, *Genealogical and Personal History of Lycoming County, Pennsylvania,* Williamsport: Frank H. Painter, 1939.

Eastman, Frank M., *Courts and Lawyers of Pennsylvania (1623-1923),* 3 vols., New York: American Historical Society, Inc., 1922.

Eckenrode, H. J., *Rutherford B. Hayes, Statesman of Reunion,* New York: Dodd, Mead & Co., 1930.

Eder, William, *A Memoir of Henry C. Carey*, Philadelphia: American Iron and Steel Association, 1880.

Funk, Arthur Lee, *Life and Works of Henry Charles Carey* (Typewritten Thesis, The Pennsylvania State College), 1925.

Green, Arnold W., *Henry Charles Carey*, Philadelphia: University of Pennsylvania, 1951.

Grossman, Jonathan, *William Sylvis, Pioneer of American Labor*, New York: Columbia University, 1945.

Haynes, Frederick E., *James Baird Weaver*, Iowa City, Iowa: State Historical Society of Iowa, 1919.

Holzman, Robert S., *Stormy Ben Butler*, New York: Macmillan Co., 1954.

Jordan, John W. et al., *Encyclopedia of Pennsylvania Biography*, New York: Lewis Historical Publishing Company, 1915.

———, *A History of Delaware County, Pennsylvania, and Its People*, New York: Lewis Historical Publishing Company, 1914.

———, *A History of the Juniata Valley and Its People*, New York: Lewis Historical Publishing Company, 1913.

Kaplan, Abraham D. H., *Henry Charles Carey*, Baltimore: Johns Hopkins Press, 1931.

Kulp, George B., *Wyoming Valley*, 2 vols., Wilkes-Barre: George B. Kulp, 1889.

Larson, Henrietta M., *Jay Cooke, Private Banker*, Cambridge: Harvard University Press, 1936.

McCrane, Reginald C., *William Allen, A Study in Western Democracy*, Columbus: F. J. Heer, 1925.

Mack, Edward C., *Peter Cooper, Citizen of New York*, New York: Duell, Sloan, and Pearce, 1949.

Meginness, John F., *Biographical Annals of Deceased Residents of The West Branch Valley of the Susquehanna, from the Earliest Times to the Present*, Williamsport: Gazette and Bulletin, 1889.

Powderly, Terence V., *Thirty Years of Labor—1859-1889*, Columbus: Excelsior Publishing House, 1891.

Schlegel, Marvin W., *Life of Franklin B. Gowen, Ruler of the Reading*, Harrisburg: Archives Publishing Co., 1947.

Schlesinger, Arthur M., Jr., *The Age of Jackson*, Boston: Little, Brown and Co., 1945.

Smith, Percy J., *Notable Men of Pittsburgh and Vicinity*, Pittsburgh: Pittsburgh Printing Co., 1901.

Twentieth Century Bench and Bar of Pennsylvania, 2 vols., Chicago: H. C. Cooper, Jr., Bro. & Co., 1903.

Williamson, Leland M., *Prominent and Progressive Pennsylvanians of the Nineteenth Century*, Philadelphia: Record Publishing Company, 1898.

MONOGRAPHS, MONOGRAPHIC ARTICLES AND TREATISES

A Century and Ten Years of Farm Production in Pennsylvania, Bulletin 49, The Pennsylvania State College Agricultural Extension Service, State College, Pa., 1953.

Barrett, Don C., *The Greenbacks and Resumption of Specie Payments, 1862-1879,* Cambridge: Harvard Union Press, 1931.

Beard, Charles A., *An Economic Interpretation of the Constitution of United States,* New York: Macmillan Co., 1915.

——, Mary R., *A Short History of the American Labor Movement,* New York: Macmillan Co., 1924.

Berkey, William A., *The Money Question,* Grand Rapids, Michigan: W. W. Hart, 1876.

Billington, Ray D., *Westward Expansion,* New York: Macmillan Co., 1940.

Bolles, Albert S., *Financial History of the United States, 1861-1885,* New York: Appleton and Co., 1880.

Briggs, Samuel D., *The National Currency: Our Financial Troubles and Their Remedy,* New York: John J. Canlon, 1873.

Buck, Solon J., *The Agrarian Crusade,* New Haven: Yale University Press, 1920.

"Henry C. Carey," in *Nation* (October 16, 1879).

Clark, Victor S., *History of Manufacturing in the United States, 1860-1914,* New York: McGraw-Hill, 1929.

Destler, Chester M., *American Radicalism (1865-1901) Essays and Documents,* New London, Conn.: Connecticut College, 1946.

——, "The Origin and Character of the Pendleton Plan," in *Mississippi Valley Historical Review,* XXIV (September 1931), 171-184.

Dewey, Davis, *Financial History of the United States,* New York: Longmans, Green and Co., 1922.

——, *State Banking Before the Civil War,* Senate Document 581, Vol. 34, Washington, D. C.: Government Printing Office, 1910.

Dewees, Frank P., *Molly Maguires: The Origin, Growth, and Character of the Organization,* Philadelphia: J. B. Lippincott Co., 1877.

Dorfman, Joseph, *The Economic Mind in American Civilization,* 3 vols., New York: Viking Press, 1946.

Dulles, Foster R., *Labor in America,* New York: T. G. Crowell Co., 1949.

Eaton, Dorman B., *The Independent Movement in New York,* New York: G. P. Putnam, 1880.

Fine, Nathan, *Labor and Farmer Parties in the United States, 1828-1928,* New York: Rand School of Social Science, 1933.

Foner, Philip S., *History of the Labor Movement in the United States,* New York: International Publishers, 1947.

Ford, Henry J., *The Rise and Growth of American Politics,* New York: Macmillan Co., 1898.

Geary, Sister M. Theophane, *A History of Third Parties in Pennsylvania, 1840-1860,* Washington, D. C.: The Catholic University Press, 1938.

Harris, Herbert, *American Labor,* New Haven: Yale University Press, 1938.

Haynes, Frederick E., *Third Party Movements Since the Civil War,* Iowa City, Iowa: State Historical Society of Iowa, 1916.

Hedges, Joseph E., *Commercial Banking and the Stock Market before 1863,* Baltimore: Johns Hopkins Press, 1938.

Helfman, Harold M., "The Liberal Republican Revolt of 1872 and the Oil Regions," in *Western Pennsylvania Historical Magazine*, XXXIII (September-December, 1950), 111-124.

Hepburn, A. Barton, *History of Coinage and Currency of the United States*, New York: Macmillan Co., 1903.

Hibbard, Benjamin H., *A History of Public Land Policies*, New York: Macmillan Co., 1924.

Hicks, John D., *The Populist Revolt*, Minneapolis: University of Minnesota Press, 1931.

Hill, William F., *The Grange Movement in Pennsylvania*, Chambersburg: Pennsylvania Grange News, 1923.

Hofstadter, Richard, *The American Political Tradition*, New York: Alfred A. Knopf, 1951.

Holdsworth, James T. and Dewey, Davis R., *The First and Second Banks of the United States*, Washington, D. C.: Government Printing Office, 1910.

Josephson, Matthew, *The Politicos, 1865-1896*, New York: Harcourt, Brace & Co., 1938.

Kellogg, Edward, *Labor and Other Capital: The Rights of Each Secured and the Wrongs of Both Eradicated. Or, an exposition of the cause why few are wealthy and many poor, and the delineation of a system, which, without infringing the rights of property, will give to labor its just reward,* New York: Edward Kellogg, 1849.

Kent, Frank R., *The Democratic Party, A History*, New York: The Century Co., 1928.

Kinley, David, *The Independent Treasury of the United States and Its Relations to the Banks of the Country*, Senate Document 587, Vol. 38, Washington, D. C.: Government Printing Office, 1910.

Knox, John J., *A History of the Various Issues of Paper Money*, New York: Charles Scribner's Sons, 1884.

Libby, Orin G., "A Study of the Greenback Movement, 1876-1884," in Wisconsin Academy of Sciences, Arts and Letters, *Transactions*, XII (Madison, 1898), pp. 530-543.

McClure, Alexander K., *Old Time Notes of Pennsylvania*, Philadelphia: Winston and Co., 1905.

McGrane, Reginald C., "Ohio and the Greenback Movement," in *Mississippi Valley Historical Review*, XI, Proceedings (March, 1925), 526-542.

Miller, Henry, *Banking Theories in the United States before 1860*, Cambridge: Harvard University Press, 1927.

Mitchell, Wesley C., *Gold Prices and Wages Under the Greenback Standard*, Berkeley: The University of California Press, 1908.

————, *History of the Greenbacks—1862-1865*, Chicago: University of Chicago Press, 1903.

Myers, Margaret C., *The New York Money Market: Origins and Development*, New York: Columbia University Press, 1931.

Perlman, Selig, *A History of Trade Unionism in the United States*, New York: A. M. Kelley, 1922.

Redlich, Fritz, *The Molding of American Banking: Men and Ideas, 1781-1840*, New York: The Hafner Co., 1947.

Ruggles, Clyde O., "The Economic Basis of the Greenback Movement in Iowa and Wisconsin," in *Mississippi Valley Historical Review*, VI, *Proceedings* (Lincoln, Nebr., 1912-1913), 142-165.

Schattschneider, Elmer E., *Party Government*, New York: Farrar & Rinehart, 1942.

Shannon, Fred A., *The Farmer's Last Frontier—Agriculture, 1860-1897*, New York and Toronto: Farrar & Rinehart, 1945.

Shipley, Max, *The Greenback Issue in the Old Northwest*, Chicago: University of Illinois Press, 1929.

Shultz, William J. and Caine, M. R., *Financial Development of the United States*, New York: Prentice-Hall, 1937.

Sparks, Edward T., *History and Theory of Agricultural Credit in the United States*, New York: T. Y. Crowell Co., 1952.

Spaulding, Elbridge G., *A Resource of War*, Buffalo, New York. Express Printing Company, 1869.

Sprague, Oliver M. W., *History of Crises Under the National Banking System*, Washington: Government Printing Office, 1910.

Stanwood, Edward, *A History of the Presidency*, New York: Houghton Mifflin Co., 1916.

Taus, Esther R., *Central Banking Function of the United States Treasury (1789-1941)*, New York: Columbia University Press, 1943.

Taussig, Frank W., *Tariff History of the United States*, New York: G. P. Putnam, 1931.

Theiss, Lewis E., "Lumbering in Penn's Woods," in *Pennsylania History*, XIX (October, 1952), 397-412.

Types of Farming in Pennsylvania, Bulletin 479, The Pennsylania State College Agricultural Experiment Station, State College, Pa., 1946.

Usher, Ellis B., *The Greenback Movement of 1875-1884 and Wisconsin's Part in It*, Milwaukee: Weisenheimer Printing Co., 1911.

Vickers, George, *The Fall of Bossism: History of Reform Movement in Philadelphia and Pennsylvania*, Philadelphia: The Bryson Co., 1883.

Ware, Norman J., *The Labor Movement in the United States, 1860-1895*, New York: D. Appleton and Co., 1929.

Warren, George F. and Pearson, Frank A., *Gold and Prices*, New York: John Wiley and Sons, 1935.

Watson, David K., *History of American Coinage*, New York: G. P. Putnam Co., 1899.

Woodruff, Clinton R., *Primary Elections in Pennsylvania*, Chicago: The Hollister Co., 1898.

Zachos, John C., *The Political and Financial Opinions of Peter Cooper*, New York: Trow's Printing Company, 1877.

APPENDIX A

The United States, by reason of its vast territory, fertile soil, varied productions, rich minerals, and temperate climate, could, wisely governed, sustain in comfort and even luxury a population tenfold greater than at present occupy it. Nevertheless, with an enterprising, industrious people, after a series of abundant harvest, manufacturers are idle, business prostrate, labor unemployed and starvation impending. This condition of affairs has been produced by the control of the producing interests of the country by the non-producer and by legislation in favor of non-productive capital and as against the interest of the laborer of the country. The policy adopted has reduced the value of property, public and private, over one-half, whilst National, State, municipal, and private debts nominally the same, have, by reason of such reduction, practically doubled.

From such policy bankruptcy of the producing interests has been the natural and inevitable result. For such control both the Republican and Democratic parties are responsible, and the wisdom of such policy has been affirmed by the Republicans at Cincinnati and the Democrats at St. Louis, and by both parties in their State platforms adopted in Pennsylvania. Wisdom would dictate as a remedy for existing evils not only the repeal of pernicious laws and the establishment of a wise and judicious financial system, framed in the interest of the productive labor of the country, but also the condemnation of the people manifested at the ballot-box, of the Democratic and Republican parties, by whom the producing interests of the country have been betrayed; therefore it is

Resolved, That neither the Democratic nor Republican parties of the country are entitled to the confidence of the people or worthy of their support, and that their record in the past has been such as to render any pledge they may make in the future as unreliable and unworthy of credit, to be regarded as pledges made under fear of public wrath, to be unredeemed if by reason of such pledges public indignation is allayed.

Resolved, That we reaffirm and indorse the platform of principles adopted by the Toledo National Convention on the 22nd day of February, 1878.

Resolved, That as the power to create money is the highest prerogative of government, and as upon the regulation of the volume and value of such money, by wise and judicious legislation, depend the prosperity and welfare of the nation, such power should be jealously guarded and controlled, and no power to regulate either its volume or value should be given to banks or other moneyed corporation which by reason of such power could subserve private ends and at will contract or expand the currency of the country and thus hold all producing and laboring interest in absolute bondage.

Resolved, That the present national banking system is not only burdensome to the people by reason of the substitution of an inferior currency for money at a heavy expense to the country in the useless payment of interest on bonds, but by reason of the power in them such banks are obtaining permanent control of the government and are becoming the absolute master of all the business interests of the country, and that in the interests of the manufacturer, farmer, the mechanic and the laborer national bank currency should be withdrawn from circulation and full legal-tender money substituted by the government in lieu thereof.

Resolved, That as the wealth of the nation is founded upon labor, the laborer should be protected in his just rights. It is desirable that the hours of labor should be so limited as to afford the laborer an opportunity to cultivate his mental faculties and enjoy rational social intercourse with his friends. To earn such reasonable wages as may be an equitable proportion of the profits of his industry, and this so that he may ameliorate his condition and obtain the comforts and luxuries of life, and thus, by increasing consumption, open new avenues for industry and new fields for labor. To educate his children, and thus, through universal education, elevate labor and the character of the laborer. For the purpose of attaining these ends.

Resolved, That the prison contract system should be prohibited; that the Federal and State Governments and municipal corporations should limit the hours of labor; that the manufacturing, mining and farming, and laborers' interests of the country be protected:

First. By lowering the rate of interest on money and effecting this by the government issuing full legal-tender money sufficient for the wants of trade and regulating its value and its volumes by wise and judicious legislation.

Second. By the protection of American industries by the enactment of a tariff based on constitutional limits for revenue, but with discrimination for protection to the labor of the farmer, the miner, the manufacturer and the producing interests.

Third. By holding public lands for the use of the actual settler, and not to be granted as subsidies have been so granted; to hold such corporations to a strict accountability, and where the terms of the grant have not been complied with to reclaim such lands as having been forfeited and as having reverted to the government.

Fourth. By opening new fields for labor in the construction of works of national importance, either directly by the government itself or by rendering assistance, in no case to be in the form of subsidies, but all outlays of the government to be adequately secured.

Fifth. By encouraging our ship-building interests and the carrying of American products in American ships, and to render such aid under proper guarantees against fraud as will enable American steamships to compete with foreign lines.

Sixth. To afford a safe depository for money and to protect the people against the fraud and loss occasioned by savings banks and trust companies, a postal depository system should be established, from which, upon being deposited, certificates of deposit bearing a low rate of interest should be payable on demand in full legal-tender government money.

Seventh. That we demand the repeal by the State government of all charters and special privileges inconsistent with the present Constitution of the State, the damage, if any, when judicially ascertained, to be paid by the State.

Eighth. That we demand the passage and enforcement of such laws as will prevent all combinations, discriminations or granting of rebates by transportation companies, and compelling common carriers to furnish the same facilities and perform the same price to all men.

Ninth. That we demand the immediate repeal of the resumption act of 1875.

Tenth. That we demand equal and just taxation of all property whatsoever, except that used by the Federal Government and used or held for government purposes.

Eleventh. That we demand the payment of government bonds according to the original contract, in the lawful money of the nation.

Resolved, That to significantly designate our State organization, designed to secure financial and labor reform, we adopt the name of National-Greenback-Labor party of Pennsylvania.

Whereas, The struggles of seven centuries for civil liberty have, in this country, culminated in securing to all an equal right to the ballot; and whereas, we believe the intelligent and honest exercise of this privilege, judiciously directed the finances of the country, will secure general prosperity through a more equitable distribution of the products of labor; therefore,

Resolved, That this convention condemns all lawlessness, violence of disorder to accomplish its ends, believing that the happiness of the whole people can only be permanently secured through the ballot after a calm, free, open, and searching discussion of the grave questions which press themselves upon the convention.[1]

[1] Philadelphia *Times,* May 10, 1878.

APPENDIX B

The National Greenback-Labor Platform Adopted at Chicago, Illinois, June 10, 1880[1]

Civil government should guarantee the divine right of every laborer to the results of his toil, thus enabling the producers of wealth to provide themselves with the means for physical comfort, and the facilities for mental, social, and moral culture; and we condemn as unworthy of our civilization the barbarism which imposes upon the wealth producers a state of perpetual drudgery as the price of bare animal existence. Notwithstanding the enormous increase of productive power, the universal introduction of labor-saving machinery, and the discovery of new agents for the increase of wealth, the task of the laborer is scarcely lightened, the hours of toil are but little shortened, and few producers are lifted from poverty into comfort and pecuniary independence. The associated monopolies, the international syndicates, and other income classes demand dear money and cheap labor: "a strong government," and hence a weak people.

Corporate control of the volume of money has been the means of dividing society into hostile classes, if the unjust distribution of the products of labor, and of building up monopolies of associated capital endowed with power to confiscate private property. It has kept money scarce, and scarcity of money enforces debt, trade, and public and corporate loans. Debt engenders usury, and usury ends in the bankruptcy of the borrower. Other results are deranged markets, uncertainty in manufacturing enterprise and agriculture, precarious and intermittent employment for the laborers, industrial war, increasing pauperism and crime and the consequent intimidation and disfranchisement of the producer, and a rapid declension into economic feudalism: therefore, we declare—

1. That the right to make and issue money is a sovereign power, to be maintained by the people for the common benefit. The delegation of this right to corporations is a surrender of the central attribute of sovereignty, void of constitutional sanction, conferring upon a subordinate, irresponsible power absolute dominion over industry and commerce. All money, whether metallic or paper, should be issued and its volume controlled by the Government, and not by or through banking corporations, and, when so issued, should be full legal tender for all debts public and private.

2. That the bonds of the United States should not be refunded, but paid as rapidly as practicable, according to contract. To enable the Government to meet these obligations, legal-tender currency should be substituted for the notes of the national banks, the national bank-

[1] Appletons' *Annual Cyclopaedia*, 1880, 696.

ing system abolished, and the unlimited coinage of silver, as well as gold, established by law.

3. That labor should be so protected by National and State authority as to equalize its burdens and insure a just distribution of its results. The eight-hour law of Congress should be enforced, the sanitary conditions of industrial establishments placed under rigid control, the competition of contract convict-labor abolished, a bureau of labor statistics established, factories, mines, and workshops inspected, the employment of children under fourteen years of age forbidden, and wages paid in cash.

4. Slavery being simply cheap labor, and cheap labor being simply slavery, the importation and presence of Chinese serfs necessarily tends to brutalize and degrade American labor; therefore, immediate steps should be taken to abrogate the Burlingame treaty.

5. Railroad land-grants forfeited by reason of non-fulfillment of contract should be immediately reclaimed by the Government, and henceforth the public domain reserved as homes for actual settlers.

6. It is the duty of Congress to regulate interstate commerce. All lines of communication and transportation should be brought under such legislative control as shall secure moderate, fair, and uniform rates for passenger and freight traffic.

7. We denounce as destructive to prosperity and dangerous to liberty the action of the old parties in fostering and sustaining gigantic land, railroad, and money corporations and monopolies, invested with and exercising powers belonging to the Government, and yet not responsible to it for the manner of their exercise.

8. That the Constitution, in giving Congress the power to borrow money, to declare war, to raise and support armies, to provide and maintain a nation, never intended that the men who loaned their money for an interest consideration should be preferred to the soldiers and sailors who periled their lives and shed their blood on land and sea in defense of their country; and we condemn the cruel class legislation of the Republican party, which, while professing great gratitude to the soldier, has most unjustly discriminated against him in favor of the bondholder.

9. All property should bear its just proportion of taxation, and we demand a graduated income-tax.

10. We denounce as most dangerous the efforts everywhere to restrict the right of suffrage.

11. We are opposed to an increase of the standing army in time of peace, and the insidious scheme to establish an enormous military power under the guise of military laws.

12. We demand absolute democratic rules for the government of Congress, placing all representatives of the people upon an equal foot-

ing, and taking away from committees a veto power greater than that of the President.

13. We demand a government of the people, by the people, and for the people, instead of a government of the bondholder, by the bondholder, and for the bondholder; and we denounce every attempt to stir up strife as an effort to conceal monstrous crimes against the people.

14. In the furtherance of these ends we ask the cooperation of all fair-minded people. We have no quarrel with individuals, wage no war upon classes, but only against vicious institutions. We are not content to endure further discipline from our present actual rulers, who, having dominion over money, over transportation, over land and labor, and largely over the press and machinery of government wield unwarrantable power over our institutions and over life and property.